ANXIETY DISORDERS:
A SCIENTIFIC APPROACH
FOR SELECTING THE
MOST EFFECTIVE TREATMENT

Samuel Knapp, EdD
Harrisburg, Pennsylvania

Leon VandeCreek, PhD
Department of Psychology
Indiana University of Pennsylvania

Professional Resource Press
Sarasota, Florida

Published by
Professional Resource Press
(An imprint of the Professional Resource Exchange, Inc.)
Post Office Box 15560
Sarasota, FL 34277-1560

Printed in the United States of America

Portions of this book first appeared in *Diagnosis and Treatment Selection for Anxiety Disorders* by S. Knapp and L. VandeCreek, Copyright © 1989 by Professional Resource Exchange, Inc.

The copy editor for this book was Patricia Hammond, the managing editor was Debra Fink, the production coordinator was Laurie Girsch, and the cover designer was Bill Tabler.

The views expressed in this guide do not necessarily represent those of the Pennsylvania Psychological Association.

Library of Congress Cataloging-in-Publication Data

Knapp, Samuel.
    Anxiety disorders : a scientific approach for selecting the most effective treatment / Samuel Knapp, Leon VandeCreek.
       p. cm. -- (Practitioner's resource series)
    Includes bibliographical references.
    ISBN 1-56887-000-0
    1. Anxiety. 2. Phobias. 3. Obsessive-compulsive disorder.
I. VandeCreek, Leon. II. Title. III. Series.
RC531.K577 1994
616.85'223--dc20
                          94-7201
                          CIP

PREFACE TO THE SERIES

As a publisher of books, cassettes, and continuing education programs, the Professional Resource Press and Professional Resource Exchange, Inc. strive to provide mental health professionals with highly applied resources that can be used to enhance clinical skills and expand practical knowledge.

All the titles in the *Practitioner's Resource Series* are designed to provide important new information on topics of vital concern to psychologists, clinical social workers, marriage and family therapists, psychiatrists, and other mental health professionals.

Although the focus and content of each book in this series will be quite different, there will be notable similarities:

1. Each title in the series will address a timely topic of critical clinical importance.
2. The target audience for each title will be practicing mental health professionals. Our authors were chosen for their ability to provide concrete "how-to-do-it" guidance to colleagues who are trying to increase their competence in dealing with complex clinical problems.
3. The information provided in these books will represent "state-of-the-art" information and techniques derived from both clinical experience and empirical research. Each of these guide books will include references and resources for those who wish to pursue more advanced study of the discussed topic.

4. The authors will provide numerous case studies, specific recommendations for practice, and the types of "nitty-gritty" details that clinicians need before they can incorporate new concepts and procedures into their practices.

We feel that one of the unique assets of the Professional Resource Press is that all of its editorial decisions are made by mental health professionals. The publisher, all editorial consultants, and all reviewers are practicing psychologists, marriage and family therapists, clinical social workers, and psychiatrists.

If there are other topics you would like to see addressed in this series, please let me know.

Lawrence G. Ritt, Publisher

ABSTRACT

This guide presents current information on diagnosis and treatment selection for anxiety disorders. Each anxiety disorder listed in *DSM-III-R* and *DSM-IV* is described and the latest research on differential diagnosis and frequent diagnostic complications and coexisting disorders is considered. Explicit decision rules are provided for treatment selection based on empirical research and clinical judgment. Specific psychological tests are recommended to supplement treatment interviews. Sample case vignettes are provided to illustrate the more common anxiety disorders. Although details on how to implement specific techniques are not provided, training materials are referenced for readers who want more information about treatment strategies. Also included are copies of several questionnaires and inventories that are frequently used in the assessment of anxiety disorders.

TABLE OF CONTENTS

ANXIETY DISORDERS: A SCIENTIFIC APPROACH FOR SELECTING THE MOST EFFECTIVE TREATMENT

INTRODUCTION

The diagnosis and treatment of anxiety disorders have changed extensively in the past 20 years and especially in the last few years. Most of these changes have occurred because of the demonstrated effectiveness of behavioral and pharmacological treatments. Treatments that were experimental or novel 20 years ago are now part of standard treatment regimens. These treatments include the use of graduated exposure with panic disorders, response prevention and clomipramine with obsessive-compulsive disorders, and the use of antidepressants and alprazolam (Xanax) to suppress panic attacks. Some older treatments now are being applied with more success with other anxiety disorders. For example, psychoanalytic procedures, which had a poor track record with anxiety disorders, are being modified on the basis of recent information to make them more effective.

The third edition of the *Diagnostic and Statistical Manual of Mental Disorders* (*DSM-III*; American Psychiatric Association, 1980) provided more precise descriptions and criteria for diagnoses of anxiety disorders than previous editions. The *DSM-III* eliminated the overly broad diagnosis of "anxiety state" and created the more specific diagnoses of generalized anxiety disorder, agoraphobia with panic disorder, agoraphobia without panic

1

disorder, panic disorder, social phobia, specific phobia, and post-traumatic stress disorder. The *DSM-III* also provided reliable operational criteria to distinguish these diagnostic categories. This standardization allowed researchers to compare studies across a wide range of treatment settings and procedures.

The 1987 revision of the *DSM-III*, the *DSM-III-R* (American Psychiatric Association, 1987), used empirical research to further refine psychiatric diagnoses.

In 1994, the *DSM-IV* (American Psychiatric Association, 1994) was released. Although *DSM-IV* provides some refinements within the different diagnostic categories, it retains the basic classification system found in *DSM-III-R*. A major change in the *DSM-IV* is the identification of a Mixed Anxiety-Depressive Disorder diagnosis. We discuss this disorder briefly at the end of the introduction. However, we do not believe that this disorder, as of yet, has the empirical data sufficient to warrant a separate classification or to guide treatment interventions.

Table 1 (p. 3) outlines the major differences between the *DSM-III*, the *DSM-III-R,* and the *DSM-IV* for anxiety disorders.

In addition, the *DSM-III-R* and *DSM-IV* abolish most hierarchical rules. The hierarchical rules of the *DSM-III* required the clinician to follow a predetermined sequence in making a diagnosis. For example, if a patient presented symptoms of depression and panic disorder under the *DSM-III*, then the diagnosis would be depression because the hierarchical rules required that the depression diagnosis take precedence over the panic disorder. However, anxiety disorders have high co-morbidity with each other and with other nonanxiety disorders, and under the *DSM-III-R* and *DSM-IV* rules, these additional diagnoses are now recognized.

The *DSM-III* and especially the *DSM-III-R* and *DSM-IV* helped clarify the diagnosis of personality disorders which often coexist with anxiety disorders. The identification of a coexisting personality disorder greatly aids in the total treatment of the anxiety patient.

The changes included in the *DSM-III-R* and *DSM-IV* are consistent with current research on the differentiation of anxiety disorders. Table 2 (pp. 4-5) summarizes several demographic and clinical variables that characterize the different anxiety disorders.

**TABLE 1: COMPARISON OF *DSM-III*, *DSM-III-R*, AND
DSM-IV CATEGORIES OF ANXIETY DISORDERS**

DSM-III	*DSM-III-R*	*DSM-IV*
Agoraphobia with panic attacks	Panic disorder with agoraphobia	Panic disorder with agoraphobia
Panic disorder	Panic disorder without agoraphobia	Panic disorder without agoraphobia
Agoraphobia without panic attacks	Agoraphobia without history of panic disorder	Agoraphobia without history of panic disorder
Social phobia	Social phobia	Social phobia
Specific phobia	Specific phobia	Specific phobia
Obsessive-compulsive disorder	Obsessive-compulsive disorder	Obsessive-compulsive disorder
Generalized anxiety disorder	Generalized anxiety disorder	Generalized anxiety disorder
Post-traumatic stress disorder	Post-traumatic stress disorder	Post-traumatic stress disorder
Atypical anxiety disorder	Anxiety disorder not otherwise specified	Anxiety disorder not otherwise specified
		Acute stress disorder
		Anxiety disorder due to general medical condition
		Substance-induced anxiety disorder

TABLE 2: DEMOGRAPHIC AND CLINICAL VARIABLES ASSOCIATED WITH ANXIETY DISORDERS

	Mean Age of Onset[a]	Prevalence per 100 Population[c]	Sex Ratio[a]	Familial Pattern	Reliability of Diagnosis[d]	Sodium Lactate Reaction	Antidepressant Response	Complications
Specific Phobia	varies widely	2.5	F > M	high	.47	no	no	Generalized Anxiety Disorder
Social Phobia	16 (9)[b]	1.5	F = M	unknown	.77	no	no	depression d & a[f] avoidant pd[g]
Panic Disorder	27 (12)	3	F = M	high	.69	yes	yes	depression
Agora-phobia	26 (9)	6	F > M	high	.85	yes	yes	depression avoidant and dependent pd[g] d & a[f]

Generalized Anxiety Disorder	23 (12)	3	F = M	low	.47	no	no	other anxiety disorders
Obsessive-Compulsive Anxiety	26 (15)	2.5[h]	F > M	high	.66	no	sometimes	depression other anxiety disorders compulsive pd[g]
Post-Traumatic Stress Disorder	varies widely	varies	varies	low	.86[e]	no	sometimes	depression d & a[f]

[a]Thyer, Parrish, et al. (1985).
[b]Numbers in parentheses beside ages refer to standard deviations.
[c]Reich (1986).
[d]DiNardo et al. (1983).
[e]Blanchard et al. (1986).
[f]d & a = drug or alcohol abuse.
[g]pd = personality disorder.
[h]Rasmussen and Eisen, 1992.

THE INITIAL ASSESSMENT

The initial interviewing process should follow a funneling procedure in which the psychotherapist begins by developing a broad picture of the patient's problems and gradually narrows them to more specific problems. In this initial phase, the psychotherapist should learn the patient's perceptions of problem areas and his or her specific assets.

A comprehensive assessment should meet three major objectives: describe the presenting problem, aid in the selection of optimal treatment, and provide a means for evaluating treatment outcome. The traditional diagnostic label largely fulfills the first goal of describing the patient's problem. A diagnosis, however, is often not sufficient to choose an optimal treatment. More information will usually have to be collected to complete the treatment selection stage. Similarly, the diagnostic label does not provide enough information to direct psychotherapists in the treatment evaluation stage. In the evaluation stage psychotherapists often rely on formal tests or behavioral measures such as diaries that record the frequency of panic attacks (for panic disorder patients, for example), rituals performed (for obsessive-compulsive patients), or participation in feared social interactions (for social phobics). Many psychotherapists also use more formal psychological tests to evaluate the overall emotional functioning of a client.

THE USE OF PSYCHOLOGICAL TESTS

Many psychotherapists rely on formal psychological tests and questionnaires to help in making treatment decisions. Others limit their use to those directly relevant to the patient's presenting complaint. Only psychotherapists who have received formal training in psychometric theory and test interpretation should use formal psychological tests. Others should refer for psychological testing when needed. In later sections we provide examples of how test profiles can improve treatment planning.

The Life History Questionnaire. This questionnaire (Lazarus, 1976) elicits information on general problem areas, the patient's self-concept, the degree of distress, personal assets, and life history.

The Beck Depression Inventory. Depression is such a common coexisting or secondary problem to anxiety disorders that psychotherapists should routinely screen anxiety disorder patients for depression. The Beck Depression Inventory (BDI), the most frequently used measure of depression (Beck et al., 1961), is now published by the Psychological Corporation. It assesses 21 symptoms including pessimism, sense of failure, dissatisfaction, self-accusations, suicidal ideas, indecisiveness, and somatic preoccupation. Psychotherapists may find items dealing with cognitive factors especially helpful for identifying demoralization secondary to the anxiety disorder, and the items dealing with vegetative symptoms such as loss of appetite, weight loss, and loss of libido can be suggestive of primary depression.

The BDI is either self-administered (10-15 minutes) or read to the patient. Each item has four or five possible responses, and each response is weighted between 0 and 3. Total scores range from 0 to 63. Scores in the range of 11 to 20 indicate mild to borderline depression, 21 to 30 indicate moderate depression, and scores over 30 define severe depression.

Other Measures. Global personality measures such as the MMPI or projective testing are not usually necessary. These tests may, however, be helpful if the initial screening yields ambiguous or complicated findings and if more information about the patient is desired. Behavioral diaries (Michelson, 1987) can be useful as diagnostic and treatment evaluation devices.

Table 3 (p. 8) displays average scores on commonly used assessment tools obtained by patients in various diagnostic categories. Table 3 contains scores from the BDI, the Fear Questionnaire (FQ; Marks & Matthews, 1979), and the State-Trait Anxiety Inventory, Trait version (STAI; Spielberger, Gorsuch, & Lushene, 1970). The FQ is a common assessment tool for social phobics and agoraphobics and is described in detail in the section entitled "Obsessive-Compulsive Disorders" (pp. 43-52). The STAI is commonly used to assess trait anxiety. Although we do not describe it in detail in the following sections, its scores are listed here to provide another scale for comparison of the anxiety disorders.

OVERVIEW OF TREATMENT TECHNIQUES

This guide deals primarily with diagnosing anxiety disorders and selecting treatment. Although we do not provide comprehensive details about how to implement treatment techniques, this section does give an overview of treatment techniques commonly used for anxiety disorders with references for training materials. Readers are advised to acquire supervised training in the use of each of these techniques before implementing them.

TABLE 3: SAMPLE ASSESSMENT SCORES FOR ANXIETY DISORDERS

	BDI[a] Scores	FQ (Social Subscale)	FQ (Agoraphobia Subscale)	STAI[a] (Trait)
Specific Phobia	15 (9)	8	9	43 (36) 41[b]
Social Phobia	12 (9)	34	6	54 (43) 51[b]
Panic Disorder	11 (18)	13	10	51 (49)
Agoraphobia	16 (17)	15	22	53 (51) 57[b]
General Anxiety Disorder	13 (23)	10	6	50 (63)
Obsessive-Compulsive Disorder	24 (25)	21	10	60 (63)
Post-Traumatic Stress Disorder	25[c]			54[c]

Note: Except as noted, all scores are from Barlow et al., 1986.

[a] Numbers in parentheses are from Turner, McCann, et al. (1986).
[b] From Cameron et al. (1986).
[c] From Fairbanks, Keane, and Malloy (1983).

Psychological treatment procedures can be divided into three general categories according to whether they address physiological (internal bodily reactions), cognitive/thinking, or interpersonal/environmental features of anxiety. No technique deals solely with one dimension, and our grouping is based on which factor seems to be primary in each of them.

Most of the therapeutic strategies suggested in this monograph have been developed out of the cognitive, behavioral, or pharmacological models because these have yielded the vast majority of process and outcome studies dealing with anxiety in the last 20 years (Sweet, Giles, & Young, 1987). Although psychotherapists may supplement these techniques by drawing on other therapeutic orientations, a detailed review of treatment manuals and outcome studies suggests that anxiety disorders are most effectively treated by using the cognitive, behavioral, or pharmacological models.

Physiological Techniques. For many patients, anxiety has a strong physiological or bodily component, often described as tension. Several relaxation procedures have been developed to reduce body tension, with progressive muscle relaxation (PMR) the most widely used (D. Bernstein & Borkovec, 1974). In PMR the patient achieves total body relaxation by tensing and relaxing various groups of muscles in a systematic order, often beginning with the feet and moving upward through the legs and abdomen to the shoulders, neck, and arms. Progressive muscle relaxation is also a primary ingredient for a number of other relaxation-based procedures such as systematic desensitization (Wolpe, 1990), in which the psychotherapist teaches patients deep muscle relaxation, then has them imagine scenes related to their phobia while in this state of relaxation. The imagined scenes are presented in a hierarchy from least to most fearful. Self-control desensitization (Goldfried & Trier, 1974), anxiety management training (Suinn, 1977), and other relaxation-based techniques also incorporate relaxation training with cognitive and interpersonal strategies (Barrios & Shigetomi, 1979; Woolfolk & Lehrer, 1984).

Flooding (Wolpe, 1990) also reduces physiological features of anxiety. Prolonged exposure to the feared situation gradually reduces the degree of anxiety. The exposure is often carried out in the patient's imagination before moving to the real situation.

When flooding was first described there was some concern that it would cause psychiatric casualties because it requires prolonged exposure to the feared situation with a high degree of anxiety. However, the clinical and research literature indicate that psychiatric casualties due to this procedure are rare (Shipley & Boudewyns, 1980).

Cognitive Techniques. According to cognitive theories, patients can reduce their dysfunctional anxiety reactions by modifying their thoughts. One popular cognitive technique involves changing irrational or unproductive beliefs. This treatment model, developed by Ellis (Whalen, DiGiuseppe, & Wessler, 1980), is called Rational-Emotive Therapy (RET). Ellis created an A-B-C model to describe how irrational thoughts might produce anxiety. In this model, activating events (A) are interpreted erroneously through dysfunctional beliefs (B) leading to unproductive consequences such as anxiety or behavioral avoidance (C). Ellis has identified 11 common irrational beliefs such as the demand that one must be perfect in all activities one performs, or the demand that one must be loved and approved by all persons. Rational-emotive therapy treatment proceeds by debunking and removing these irrational beliefs.

Beck and Emery (1985) present a similar method of altering thoughts. Beck, however, emphasizes the processes of thinking more than the content of the unproductive beliefs. For example, in Beck's model, it might be seen as a case of overgeneralized thinking if a single social rejection causes a person to shy away from other social opportunities. Beck and his associates place more emphasis on developing a positive and collaborative relationship with their patients than does Ellis, and they have presented more supportive outcome data.

Although the cognitive therapies may have a different theoretical base than behavior therapy, the two schools often employ identical or similar techniques. For example, Ellis would use systematic desensitization with certain patients. Beck incorporates many behavioral activities such as graduated exposure or gradual approximation in the treatment of anxiety (Beck & Emery, 1985).

Thought stopping is a cognitive technique (Wolpe, 1990) that stops thoughts rather than changing their content. Symptom-inducing thoughts can be interrupted through physical activities or cognitive activities which divert attention.

Guided imagery may also be used to control or reduce anxiety. During guided imagery (Lazarus, 1976) the patient practices the successful imaginal rehearsal of difficult social situations. Another technique known as paradoxical intention (Michelson & Ascher, 1984) involves reducing anticipatory anxiety by consciously trying to create the feared anxiety.

Interpersonal/Environmental Techniques. Anxiety may seriously interfere with patients' interactions with the world around them and with other people. One of the most commonly used techniques to reduce interpersonal components of anxiety is assertiveness training (Lange & Jakubowski, 1976). In the popular perception, assertiveness means "standing up for your rights." Wolpe (1990), however, defines assertiveness as the appropriate interpersonal expression of any emotion which is incompatible with anxiety. Consequently, Wolpe's procedures involve more broad-spectrum social skills training. Making friends, carrying on conversations, expressing affection, and resolving conflicts are included within Wolpe's definition of assertiveness training.

Another technique that focuses on changing the patient's relationship with the environment is response prevention (Steketee & Foa, 1985). Response prevention is used to prevent unproductive rituals or behavior linked to anxiety reduction, especially with obsessive-compulsive disorders (see commentary in the section entitled "Obsessive-Compulsive Disorders," pp. 43-52).

Graduated exposure is a technique by which patients gradually expose themselves to a feared situation. This may involve confronting an object, as in specific phobias, or going to places of perceived danger, as in panic disorder or agoraphobia (Barlow & Waddell, 1985). In addition, the treatments developed by Weekes (1969, 1976, 1984), Zane and Milt (1984), and Neuman (1985) all contain elements of graduated exposure. For example, during graduated exposure treatments, patients will deliberately place themselves in locations or situations that have previously elicited panic attacks. Furthermore, they are taught various techniques such as relaxation, somatic relabeling, or attention diversion to reduce the likelihood or severity of the panic attack. Patients are required to stay in the situation and not to leave even if they experience another panic attack. Consequently, they can break the chain between panic and avoidance of public places. Perhaps nowhere does the line between physiological, cognitive, and motoric interventions become more blurred than with graduated exposure, where cognitions are modified to change physiological reactions and increase tolerance of the phobic situation.

Relapse Prevention. The return of anxiety that had earlier been reduced is of common concern to therapists. The literature indicates that many patients experience an increase in anxiety in the months following treatment (Rachman, 1989). Research suggests that therapists can predict with some success which patients will show this type of relapse. The presence of an elevated heart rate response at the start of anxiety-reduction training strongly predicts the return of anxiety. So too is a highly demanding treatment program which generates high discomfort. In contrast, no relationship exists between return of anxiety and the amount of time taken to reduce the anxiety initially.

Relapse can be minimized or blocked by the repeated practice of fear-reducing tasks and by insuring a low level of anxiety prior to and during anxiety-reduction exercises (Rachman, 1989).

The Mixed Anxiety-Depressive Disorder (MAD). As noted in many of the forthcoming sections, depression is a secondary condition for many with anxiety disorders. This depression appears to go beyond the demoralization experienced by any person facing a chronic stressor. The frequency of coexistence of depression with anxiety has led to investigations of their relationship and speculation that the two disorders represent different manifestations of a common underlying disorder. It is also of note that some medications, especially tricyclic antidepressants (TCAs) and monoamine oxidase inhibitors (MAOIs) appear effective with both depressive and anxiety symptoms.

Interest in the relationship between depression and anxiety has led to the creation of a separate diagnostic category in *DSM-IV* called Mixed Anxiety-Depressive Disorder (MAD), which is currently being studied in field trials. The *ICD-10* (American Psychiatric Association, 1994) contains a MAD classification that refers to a syndrome with an equal mixture of subthreshold anxiety and depressive symptoms and that does not meet the diagnostic standard for any existing anxiety or depressive disorder (Boulenger & Lavallee, 1993). It is alleged that the MAD patients commonly seek treatment from primary care physicians.

The concept of MAD has its critics, however. Wittchen (cited in "Questions and Answers," 1993), for example, believes that the threshold for identifying mental illnesses is low enough. He comments: "There is a certain amount of unhappiness that goes on in life and much of it probably shouldn't be treated pharmacologically. In fact, it should be treated, if at all, psychotherapeutically" (p. 39).

The authors do not believe that the evidence of MAD has been established yet. In the absence of symptomatic and demographic data, it is premature to delineate guidelines for the identification or treatment selection for this disorder.

SPECIFIC PHOBIAS

Specific phobias (also known as simple phobias) are characterized by persistent irrational fears and avoidance of specific situations or objects. This category does not include social phobias or agoraphobias. Blood, injection, and injury (BII) phobias are classified under specific phobias within the *DSM-IV*, although we believe that they differ sufficiently from other specific phobias that they require unique treatment procedures and a separate diagnostic category (Öst, 1992; Thyer, Himle, & Curtis, 1985). These are discussed in a separate section entitled "Blood, Injection, and Injury Phobias" (pp. 18-19).

The age of onset for specific phobias varies considerably, ranging from childhood through adulthood. Phobias of animals are more likely to have their onset in childhood, while claustrophobia has an average age of onset of 20. About two-thirds of specific phobias start from a direct trauma or a series of minor traumas. Others occur through observing another person being harmed or through misinformation. The sex ratio of specific phobias is equal between men and women, except that women far exceed men in frequency of small-animal phobias.

As a group, specific phobias are less severe and debilitating than other anxiety disorders and usually do not severely limit social or occupational activities. Most persons with a limited specific phobia of, for example, snakes, can avoid snakes without seriously limiting their lives. Blood, injection, and injury phobia (BII) is an exception because the fear and avoidance of needles, dentists, or medical treatments may have significant health consequences.

Nevertheless, persons with specific phobias who present for treatment differ from persons with specific phobias in the population at large. Persons who present for treatment are more likely to have BII fears, multiple phobias, or phobias of objects or animals (e.g., dogs, elevators) that are not easily avoided (Chapman et al., 1993). Finally, many patients presenting for treatment with specific phobias have other concurrent anxiety disorders. Consequently, it is often difficult to separate the specific phobia from the other presenting problems.

DIFFERENTIAL DIAGNOSIS

Usually the self-report of the patient will be sufficient to assess the extent of the phobia. If the feared object is readily available in the natural environment, then a behavioral avoidance test may be used. The psychotherapist can use a fear thermometer (ranking anxiety on a scale of 0 to 10 with 0 = "No Anxiety" and 10 = "Extreme Anxiety") to assess the degree of anxiety.

Often specific phobias appear within a package of multiple phobias. These multiple phobias commonly develop through generalization from the original trauma. The patient who appears with multiple phobias often can identify a common theme for all the different phobias. For example, a patient involved in a vehicular accident may develop a fear of riding in vehicles, or of certain sounds associated with the operation of vehicles. The Fear Survey Schedule (Wolpe & Lang, 1969) can help to determine the degree of generalization or the extent of multiple phobias.

Specific phobias differ from Post-Traumatic Stress Disorder (PTSD) in that the phobic patient does not reexperience the event through intrusive recollections or flashbacks and does not have the extreme denial of emotional upset found in PTSD.

Specific phobias sometimes mask or coexist with other more serious mental disorders. A distinction should be made between a real phobia, which masks or coexists with other problems, and a pseudophobia, which the patient invents for an ulterior motive. Patients may "test" the psychotherapist's trustworthiness and competence by initially presenting a less threatening aspect of their pathology such as a specific phobia. A thorough social and clinical history and mental status check should identify the patient with a pseudophobia. The patient with a pseudophobia will not have the degree of upset and avoidance found with real phobias and will gradually shift to more clinically relevant topics.

TREATMENTS FOR SPECIFIC PHOBIAS

A variety of behavioral treatments have been attempted with specific phobias, including, but not limited to, systematic desensitization, *in vivo* desensitization, implosive therapy, flooding, reinforced practice, modeling (including participant and covert modeling), and cognitive therapy with exposure. These treatments are described briefly in the "Introduction" (pp. 1-13). To date, none of these techniques has demonstrated superiority over the others, although cognitive therapy without exposure may be inferior. All other strategies have the ability to reduce fears with specific phobias with a high degree of success.

No definitive research exists to predict which features of a specific phobia can best guide treatment selection from this list of possible approaches. Based on the limited literature, we prefer to select treatments on the basis of the origin of the phobia or on the ability of the patient to create imagery to evoke emotions. Although Schwartz, Davidson, and Coleman (1978) have discussed treatment selection based on mode of symptom response to the phobia (physiological, behavioral, cognitive), the research support for this as a routine approach to treatment selection is limited.

Origin of Phobia. We recommend following Wolpe's (1977, 1981, 1990) tailoring of treatments for specific phobias according to their origin. Wolpe identifies two modes of phobia onset: classical conditioning and cognitive misinformation. Wolpe believes that a different mode of onset warrants a different treatment procedure. According to Wolpe, a treatment such as systematic desensitization that is designed for the deconditioning of anxiety would not have much effect on phobic responses that require cognitive solutions.

There is no formal method of determining the mode of onset. Psychotherapists generally can ask patients about the origin of the fear and whether the original situation was perceived as dangerous. For example, a phobia of thunderstorms that developed from being caught in a serious flood or tornado would differ from one that developed out of false ideas concerning the dangers of thunderstorms. Of course, many phobias do not follow one single traumatic event, but are the result of numerous mini-traumas or anxiety-provoking experiences. Similarly, patients do not always acquire false beliefs through direct education. Sometimes persons with phobias may infer false information about the harmfulness of thunderstorms or spiders, for example, by observing the reactions of parents or others.

Some phobias are based on both direct trauma and false information. In such cases, both cognitive correction and relaxation training may be required. Airplane flight phobias are a common example of multiple causation. Although misconceptions about the safety of flying appear to cause most flight phobias, unpleasant experiences while flying, such as nausea or motion sickness during a rough flight, may produce or aggravate it as well.

Some research supports the distinction between phobias based on trauma and phobias based on false information. Wolpe's (1981) anecdotal retrospective study supported his conclusions. Also, Öst (1985) treated phobics differently according to mode of acquisition (phobias acquired vicariously were considered cognitively acquired phobias). The sample, however, included persons with social phobias, dental and blood phobias, and agoraphobia, as well as specific phobias, so it is unclear how his results should generalize to persons with specific phobias only. Although patients with conditioned fears did not respond differently to treatments (exposure, *in vivo* desensitization, or applied relaxation), those patients with cognitively based fears did better with the cognitive treatment modality (self-instructional training or fading).

Systematic desensitization and its variations are the preferred treatments with conditioned phobias. Patients with multiple phobias should have a separate hierarchy created for each phobia unless the behavior analysis shows an underlying theme or connection among the apparently different fears.

Although systematic desensitization is recommended first, different kinds of relaxation exercises besides progressive muscle relaxation (PMR) can be used. Sometimes patients have had prior experience of or interest in self-hypnosis, meditation, yoga, or biofeedback-enhanced relaxation. Wolpe (1990) also reported patients using kung fu, motoric exercises, or reading as inhibitors of anxiety. These methods of inducing relaxation can work just as well as PMR for individual patients.

In the absence of patient preferences to the contrary, however, we prefer PMR because it has a relatively low rate of negative side-effects. More patients report transient anxiety effects during the practice of meditation than during the practice of PMR. Lehrer and Woolfolk (1984) believe that the "paradoxical anxiety" is less frequent with PMR because it more directly lowers the heart rate and muscle tensions.

Ability to Utilize Imagery. A few patients cannot create imagery vivid enough for imaginal systematic desensitization to work effectively. They may have trouble evoking the images or trouble creating strong emotions out of the image. Strategies are available to increase the effectiveness of imagery, but if these fail, it may be best to use *in vivo* desensitization or flooding (Wolpe, 1990).

Mode of Response. Another perspective on treatment is based on the predominant response system, or the modified "specific-effects" hypothesis. We have reviewed the literature and the data on this perspective and do not recommend it as a routine approach for selecting treatments for specific phobias.

According to this hypothesis, all relaxation techniques produce a general relaxation response. In addition, specific treatments have specific effects superimposed upon the general relaxation state. For example, cognitive treatments are more likely to reduce cognitive anxiety, somatic treatments are more likely to reduce somatic or physiological anxiety, and behavioral treatments are more likely to reduce behavioral symptoms of anxiety such as avoidance (Schwartz et al., 1978).

Although this schema has face appeal, several problems argue against its routine application in clinical practice. First, treatments cannot be neatly categorized as cognitive, somatic, or behavioral. Systematic desensitization, for example, contains the somatic element of progressive muscle relaxation, but it also includes cognitive elements by increasing expectations of improvement and even behavioral elements when exposure to the objects in imagination may transfer to real-life exposure.

Also, the mode-of-response procedure for choosing treatments may produce contradictory results with the mode-of-acquisition schema. Some evidence suggests that classically conditioned phobias are more likely to produce physiological arousal than phobias acquired through misinformation (Öst & Hugdahl, 1981). Furthermore, psychotherapists will not always be able to classify patients as behavioral, cognitive, or physiological responders because response measures may not be sensitive to actual internal states. Physiological responses are especially difficult to measure unless psychotherapists have access to extensive recording equipment.

Finally, the evidence from outcome studies for this degree of treatment specificity has been inconsistent. For example, Öst, Johansson, and Jerremalm (1982) found that exposure was most effective with behavioral responders, while relaxation produced better outcomes with physiological responders among claustrophobia patients. Later, however, Jerremalm, Jansson, and Öst (1986) failed to find differential effectiveness for a cognitive-based over a relaxation-based treatment for differential responders suffering from dental anxiety.

In the final analysis, the research data do not support an advantage for applying treatments based on the patient's predominant mode of response. Nonetheless, psychotherapists may find individual clients who demonstrate extreme cognitive, behavioral, or physiological responses and may elect to apply differential treatments on a case-by-case basis.

BLOOD, INJECTION, AND INJURY PHOBIAS

Blood, injection, and injury (BII) phobias differ so much from specific phobias that they may warrant a separate diagnostic classification. Blood, injection, and injury phobias are classified together because they have similar demographical and clinical variables (Öst, 1992). That is, the patient first feels a typical phobic anxiety state characterized by physiological arousal, cognitions of fear, and avoidance. This is followed by a second state characterized by a decrease in physiological arousal (e.g., heart rate, blood pressure) and eventually feelings of faintness. Fainting often does occur in BII, where it does not in other specific phobias. The *DSM-IV* (American Psychiatric Association, 1994) includes BII with other specific phobias, but allows the clinician to designate it as a discrete type of specific phobia.

Most (50% to 75%) patients acquire BII phobias through direct experiences. The gender distribution is equal between men and women. Three-fifths of BII patients have other diagnoses, mostly anxiety or depression. Most developed their phobia in childhood with a mean age of onset of 8.6 years.

Some BII patients have altered vocational choices (such as leaving a career in nursing) because they could not adjust to seeing blood or receiving injections. Others will avoid participating in or watching sports, traveling to foreign countries where vaccinations are required, and donating blood, and will take other steps to avoid contact with blood, injections, or injuries. Most importantly, patients with BII will often avoid needed medical or dental care for fear of blood or injections (Öst, 1992).

Initial evidence supported a diphasic treatment plan for BII in which patients apply relaxation skills when they feel the first phase (an increase in blood pressure or heart rate). If this is successful, then the second phase will not occur. If it is not successful, and the second phase does occur, then the patient can apply tension- or anger-arousing techniques which will counteract the diphasic phase (see description in Öst & Sterner, 1987). The outcome for the diphasic treatment appears good. Subsequent research suggests that the second part of the treatment (applied tension) contains the therapeutically active ingredient for this disorder (Öst, Sterner, & Fellenius, 1989).

SOCIAL PHOBIAS

Michelle* is a 20-year-old secretary from a working-class family who has a well-paying job with a prestigious law firm. She reported feeling tense at work, and she described a strong desire to succeed on the job and to please her employers. One day at work she heard some of the

---

*Names and all identifying characteristics of persons in all vignettes have been disguised thoroughly to protect privacy.

other secretaries making sarcastic comments about her work behind her back. Afterwards Michelle became very timid and anxious around them and often stammered when she spoke. She now avoids them whenever possible. Michelle makes careless mistakes in her work whenever others are near her. Currently she is looking for a different job where she can feel more comfortable.

Michelle has a social phobia. Social phobias are persistent and irrational fears of, and the compelling desire to avoid, social situations in which the individual may be exposed to possible scrutiny by others. Persons with social phobias also fear that their behavior may result in humiliation or embarrassment. Common examples of social phobias include a fear of talking in public, of choking on food when eating in front of others, of urinating in public lavatories, or of having a hand tremble when writing in the presence of others. In some cases, the social phobia may be generalized to many social situations and include a fear of saying foolish things or of not being able to answer questions.

Marked anticipatory anxiety develops when persons suffering from this phobia are faced with the necessity of entering the feared situation. Whenever possible, they will avoid the situation, but if they are forced to endure it, they will experience intense immediate anxiety, as well as fears that others will detect signs of their discomfort. A vicious cycle often ensues in which the anxiety impairs their performance, leading to increased efforts to avoid the situation.

Although most people feel shy or embarrassed sometimes in their lives, social phobia represents a degree of fear and avoidance that substantially impairs emotional and/or behavioral functioning. Also, according to the *DSM-III-R* and *DSM-IV*, the social phobia may not be due to another psychiatric disorder. Social fear caused by paranoia, for example, is not a social phobia.

DEMOGRAPHICS

Although the age of onset for social phobia can vary considerably, it commonly begins in the late teens or early adulthood (as in the case of Michelle), when the individual begins to separate from the family of origin. Social phobias may involve some degree of constitutional predisposition as some babies appear more shy than others. However, it is probably subsequent life experiences that turn the shy baby into the socially fearful adult. The onset is often triggered by a direct trauma or a series of mini-traumas. Persons with social phobia have a high incidence of negative self-statements or irrational beliefs.

The Epidemiological Catchment Area survey found a 6-month prevalence of between 0.9% to 1.7% for men and 1.5% to 2.6% for women (Myers et al., 1984). However, the number of patients with social phobia seeking treatment is equally divided among men and women. Neal and Turner (1991) reported that the number of African-Americans seeking treatment for social phobia is low, even though they have higher rates of social phobia than white Americans. Avoidant personality disorder, which may represent an extreme variant of social phobia, was found in 0 to 1.3% of the population (Weissman, 1993).

The course of the disorder is often chronic; it rarely dissipates without treatment. Social phobias can be severe and result in greatly impaired social lives and occupational advancement. Persons with social phobia are more likely to be unmarried and to lack romantic or sexual partners.

COMPLICATIONS

In one study (Barlow, 1988), almost half of the patients with social phobia were found to have an additional diagnosis. Alcohol abuse, other anxiety disorders, and depression are especially common among patients with social phobias. Turner, Beidel, et al. (1986) found that 46% of the persons with social phobias used alcohol and 52% used anxiolytic drugs to reduce anxiety in social settings. Of course, not all of these patients had a diagnosable drug abuse disorder. Nevertheless, in alcohol treatment facilities, 25% of the men and 17% of the women had social phobias leading to speculation that the social phobia predated the alcohol disorder.

Not surprising, social phobias were commonly found to coexist with other anxiety disorders. Generalized anxiety disorders and specific phobias are especially common.

Turner, Beidel, et al. (1986) also found that about 33% of the patients with social phobia had a history of depression, and 1 in 7 had a suicidal act or gesture in their past. Similarly, Barlow (1988) found that 29% of the patients with social phobias had either dysthymic disorders or major depressions. The increased risk of depression among persons with social phobias may be due to social isolation, lack of assertiveness, the presence of common dysfunctional attitudes that they share with depressed persons, or some combination of all of the preceding factors.

Finally, Turner et al. (1991) found that 75% of patients with social phobias either had an avoidant personality disorder or sub-threshhold avoidant features. As described below, from a treatment point of view, the distinction between social phobias and avoidant personality disorder may not be useful.

DIFFERENTIAL DIAGNOSIS

Sometimes it is difficult to distinguish social phobias from panic disorders (agoraphobia). For example, both social phobics and panic disorder patients may report fears of going to restaurants, theaters, and social events. The distinction is that persons with social phobia have a fear of being with other people, whereas persons with agoraphobia fear their own spontaneous panic attacks. Although agoraphobia involves embarrassment or fear of scrutiny during a panic attack, the embarrassment is limited to actions that may occur during the panic attack and does not generalize to other social situations. These and other differences are shown in Table 4 (p. 23).

Psychotherapists must distinguish social phobias from schizoid personality disorders. Both social phobics and schizoid personality disorder patients avoid social contact. Persons with social phobia, however, would like to have social contract, but fear blocks their interactions with others. The person with schizoid personality disorder, in contrast, has no interest in others, lacks feelings of warmth and empathy, and is indifferent to praise or criticism from others.

TYPES OF SOCIAL PHOBIAS

We believe it is advantageous to distinguish between two types of social phobias based on their severity and to the extent that they involve multiple situations. We interpret recent research

TABLE 4: DIFFERENCES BETWEEN SOCIAL PHOBIA AND AGORAPHOBIA

FEATURE	SOCIAL PHOBIA	AGORAPHOBIA
Symptom Differences		
Situations Avoided	parties, social gatherings, restaurants, theaters, and so on	places where panic attacks have happened before or where they might happen; often overlaps with avoidance patterns of social phobics
Response	specific panic anticipatory anxiety	spontaneous panic anticipatory anxiety
Anticipatory Thoughts	Others will laugh at me; I will humiliate myself.	I will die; I will faint; no one will help me.
Modifiers	presence of significant other	presence of significant other
Course	mostly static	fluctuates
Complications	alcohol, drug abuse; depression; specific phobias	alcohol, drug abuse; depression; specific phobias; GAD symptoms
Demographic Features		
Age of Onset	19 (average)	26 (average)
Sex Ratio	F = M	25% male
Physiological Differences		
Sodium Lactate Response	low	high
Antidepressant Response	low (possible MAOI)	high

(e.g., Holt, Heimberg, & Hope, 1992) to suggest that social phobia exists on a continuum from a specific social phobia that involves social fear and avoidance in highly restricted situations (e.g., dating, public speaking, etc.) to a generalized social phobia that involves social fear and avoidance in a wide range of situations.

Performance anxieties such as test anxiety, public-speaking anxiety, or athletic performance anxiety are not mentioned as specific or separate diagnoses within *DSM-III-R* and *DSM-IV*, but may be mild forms of the specific social phobias mentioned previously. At times the social aspects of the performance anxiety may be subtle. Sexual performance anxiety may be due to a fear of rejection or humiliation before another person. Test anxiety may be caused by a fear of disappointing parents or humiliation with peers. Public speaking anxiety may be a highly restricted fear of public scrutiny.

Persons with the more severe generalized social phobias are more likely to have more pervasive anxiety, coexisting anxiety disorders, earlier onset, and poorer social skills than persons with specific social phobias. Avoidant personality disorder may represent an extreme social phobia that involves greatly diminished self-esteem and greatly enhanced hypersensitivity. Although the *DSM-III-R* and *DSM-IV* distinguish between social phobia and avoidant personality disorder, this distinction may be unjustified. We do not believe that this distinction is justified on the basis of clinical or empirical evidence.

Earlier research suggesting that persons with avoidant personality disorders possessed poorer social skills than social phobics may have reflected a later finding that the degree of social skills tends to deteriorate as the degree of social anxiety increases. The reason for these differences is unclear. It may be that avoidant personality disorder is more chronic and long-lasting than social phobia; thus, the avoidant individual may have lacked social opportunities to develop or practice normal social skills.

TREATMENT SELECTION WITH SOCIAL PHOBIAS

Because social phobia is a relatively newly identified disorder, most of the outcome studies involving *DSM-III-R* and *DSM-IV* criteria for social phobia have been done in recent years.

However, much research has been conducted over the past 20 years with patients who had more restricted social anxieties such as public speaking anxiety, dating anxiety, and so on. Probably many of these subjects could have met *DSM-III-R* and *DSM-IV* criteria for social phobia, but it is unknown, however, how many of these subjects had avoidant personality disorders, had general anxiety disorder, had depression, had subclinical levels of fear, or fit into other diagnostic categories.

Consequently, the research on social anxiety can be referred to, but it should be given less weight than research that has specifically involved social phobics. Research with patients with social phobias has found that social skills and cognitive behavioral treatments appear most effective. Furthermore, some outcome research has been conducted with persons with avoidant personality disorders (see review by Shea, 1993). Although the results are mixed, persons with avoidant personality disorder appear to benefit from social skills training.

The behavioral studies of social phobias and pre-*DSM-III* studies of social anxiety indicate that any of several treatments may be effective: cognitive treatments, social skills training, stress inoculation training, self-instructional training, exposure training, relaxation strategies, and anxiety management training. Although only a few of these studies were done with social phobics who met the criteria of *DSM-III-R*, many have been done with patients who were socially anxious or who had speech phobias, dating anxiety, or other social anxieties that may have some application and subject pool overlap with social phobias (see Heimberg, 1989, for a review of 17 studies that did define their subjects in terms of the criteria specified in *DSM-III* or *DSM-III-R*). In selecting treatments for social phobics, therapists should attend to the dysfunctional response systems (cognitive, physiological, or behavioral [social skills]) as well as the severity of the disorder.

Treatment Specificity. As in the treatment of specific phobias, clinicians have attempted to develop treatment specificity for social phobics. According to the multiprocess theory of relaxation and related states, different treatment strategies should impact differently depending on whether they target the cognitive, physiological, or behavioral components of the anxiety.

The studies of treatment specificity with social phobia are contradictory and full of methodological problems that defy easy interpretation. Several studies (Jerremalm et al., 1986; McCann, Woolfolk, & Lehrer, 1987; Mersh et al., 1989; Öst, Jerremalm, & Johansson, 1981; Turner & Beidel, 1985) have divided patients with social phobias into different categories based on physiological, cognitive, and/or social skills criteria. No consistent pattern has emerged and typically no difference is found through the attempts to match patient symptom patterns to treatment modalities.

Despite methodological problems and variations in outcome, it appears that nothing is lost by categorizing persons with social phobias according to predominant response mode, although clinicians should be aware that these response modes may interact in complex and idiosyncratic ways. We would try to match the client characteristics on the basis of negative cognitions, social skills, and physiological reactivity.

For example, the psychotherapist treating Michelle, described in the opening vignette, may learn that she has an excessive need to seek the approval of others. At the time of the assessment, she reported little physiological reactivity when in the phobic situation. She appears to be cooperative and eager to work on her problem. However, if her scores on assertiveness indicate that she is not assertive, and further questioning about her interactions with others supports this finding, treatment should start by altering her dysfunctional beliefs about her need to please others. Assertiveness training may also be needed.

The negative cognitions can be assessed best through interviewing, or through the Life History Questionnaire (Lazarus, 1976). The use of rationality inventories does not appear to be appropriate because they appear to measure global discomfort rather than rational thinking. Furthermore, they measure global irrationality, whereas irrational beliefs are sometimes highly specific to certain situations (Smith, 1982). Nevertheless, the psychotherapist can look for irrational beliefs or dysfunctional thinking styles (Beck & Emery, 1985) which are possible mediators of anxiety.

Social skills can be assessed through interviewing with attention to how the patient relates to the psychotherapist, and how the patient relates past social interactions and interactions with family members. Also, they can be assessed through the use of self-report assertiveness or social skills inventories. We would recommend, however, that the clinician's judgment override any test scores found with these inventories. Patients may have good social skills which are measured by these inventories, but also display social excesses (rude, inconsiderate, or inappropriate behavior) which these inventories might not identify, but would be obvious in the interviews with patients and their families.

Physiological reactivity can be harder to measure. Although researchers use equipment to measure heart rate or blood pressure in structured situations, these instruments may be beyond the resources of most psychotherapists. Furthermore, the usefulness of a single physiological measure is questioned by some researchers. Instead, it may be best to rely upon the self-report of the patient.

Treatment of Generalized Social Phobia. Research suggests that persons with specific social phobias tend to respond better to treatment than persons with more generalized social phobias or avoidant personality disorders. With more generalized social phobias and avoidant personality disorders, efforts should be made to provide longer treatment. Persons with avoidant personality disorders tend to have poorer social skills. Although they may need group therapy, it may be stressful for them and they may drop out of treatment unless special efforts are made to make the therapy comfortable for them.

Although persons with specific social phobias may be treated with a single-focus treatment according to the dominant response pattern, more comprehensive treatments are required for persons with generalized or extreme social phobia. For these patients, physiological reduction alone is unlikely to result in substantial benefit. Instead, the treatment should include a wide range of interventions including social skills training and cognitive restructuring.

Pharmacological Interventions. Pharmacological treatments show some promise, although the data do not justify giving it priority over behavioral treatments. Some studies suggest that monoamine oxidase inhibitors may help with social phobias (see reviews by Marshall, 1993, and Schneier, 1991). Also, case studies and uncontrolled reports claim that beta-adrenergic blockers (such as propranolol) reduce performance anxiety for speakers and musicians, as well as more well-defined social phobics. Beta blockers, however, do not appear effective with the more generalized social phobias.

There is at least one report that diazepam can reduce anxiety when given acutely for public speaking anxiety. The long-term effects have not been evaluated. Alprazolam may be useful for some symptoms, but the benefits have not lasted after medication was terminated.

Other medications have not yet proven their effectiveness with social phobias. Tricyclic antidepressants have not yet been found effective in the treatment of social phobias (Liebowitz et al., 1987). Studies with bupropion, buspirone, and clonidine have shown mixed results (Marshall, 1993).

Treatment Decision Summary. Currently, we would recommend first offering a behavioral program. The program can be tailored to the needs of the patient by using the behavioral, physiological, or cognitive deficiencies as assessed by the psychotherapist. We would recommend systematic or self-control desensitization for social phobias with a clear direct conditioning basis. In addition, because most socially anxious persons have some negative thoughts, it is usually necessary to do some cognitive restructuring. Social skills training may or may not be needed depending on the assessment. If the patient refuses the behavioral program or expresses a preference to try medication first, then pharmacological options can be used. Nonresponders to psychotherapy can, of course, be referred for pharmacological interventions.

A CASE VIGNETTE

Harriet is a 24-year-old graduate student in economics who is conscientious and always tries to be thoroughly prepared. She often studies her notes until she has practically memorized them. Harriet's study time is so extensive she can afford almost no social life. Still, she has found herself "worked up" over her grades. She described nervous feelings in her stomach, and she was unable to relax. According to her Life History Questionnaire, she has been this way ever since she was a sophomore in college. One day Harriet experienced a very sudden and intense nervousness while presenting a lecture on inflation to one of her graduate classes. Because of other demands on her time, she had not been able to prepare adequately. She worried about the comments and questions of the other class members and was quick to interpret them as criticisms. Although she got a grade of "B" for the lecture, she thought that the instructor was frowning and grimacing during the lecture and really did not like her presentation. Since that time, she has assiduously tried to avoid giving class presentations.

Diagnosis and Treatment Recommendations

Diagnosis.   Axis I: Social Phobia
                          Probably Generalized Anxiety Disorder
              Axis II: Not Sufficient Information

Treatment Plan. Because Harriet reported high physiological arousal, and because the fear of public speaking started with one specific situation, we would use a desensitization procedure. She probably also has generalized anxiety disorder, so we would choose self-control desensitization, which theoretically can be applied to a wide range of anxiety-producing situations. Dysfunctional cognitions related to public speaking and generalized anxiety need to be assessed through interviews to determine whether treatment should include a cognitive component. Obtaining more information about her social skills also would be helpful.

PANIC ATTACKS AND AGORAPHOBIA

Jill was an 18-year-old freshman college student who came to the Counseling Service complaining of severe anxiety. She reported sudden heart palpitations, nervousness, hyperventilation, and fear of "going crazy." She described the first episode in great detail. Since then, she has had several such "anxiety" episodes in the last month. She is now afraid of going outside without her boyfriend for fear of having another attack. A medical examination failed to find any physical reasons for her attacks.

Jill has a panic disorder. This is a complicated, confusing, and debilitating psychiatric disorder. Often, panic disorders lead to agoraphobia, or the fear of going away from places of safety. In the *DSM-III*, agoraphobia and panic disorder were considered separate diagnoses. The *DSM-III-R* and *DSM-IV*, however, consider agoraphobia as a complication of panic disorders. Typically, persons having agoraphobia proceed through two stages of development: panic attacks and then phobic avoidance or the fear of being away from places of safety.

The *DSM-III-R* established several criteria for the diagnosis of panic disorder. The panic attack must be spontaneous (not in the presence of life-endangering situations or phobic stimuli). Also, it requires that the patient experience at least four attacks in a 4-week period and that the attacks include at least 4 out of 12 possible symptoms (*DSM-IV* includes 13 possible symptoms). The possible symptoms include an increase in blood pressure, dizziness, chest pains, tachycardia, trouble breathing, trouble swallowing, paresthesia (tingling in hands or feet), hot or cold flashes, sweating, faintness, trembling, and shaking. The physical sensations differ so much from other physical states that patients often feel unreal or like they are "going crazy." Some patients may have other less common symptoms. Physiological measures of panic disorder patients verify the sudden onset and intensity of the panic attack.

The *DSM-IV* retained the division of panic disorder and panic disorder with phobic avoidance (agoraphobia). However, many clinicians believe that the descriptions of what constitutes a panic attack should be expanded to reflect the personal diversity of symptoms that could occur (Norton, Cox, & Schwartz, 1992).

The designation of four panic attacks within a 4-week period is admittedly arbitrary. These requirements were established because infrequent panic attacks occur in other diagnostic categories, and about one-third of nonpsychiatric persons experience at least one panic attack in a year. Most people, however, do not have repeated panic attacks and do not develop fear of future panic attacks.

The second phase in the development of agoraphobia is the phobic avoidance. Agoraphobic patients fear that panic attacks will recur, and consequently they restrict their movements to places such as their home, or they will go out only in the presence of a trusted person such as a spouse. Although the phobic avoidance could occur immediately after the first panic attack, the avoidance phase most often develops after repeated panic attacks over a period of months or years.

Panic disorders usually emerge between the ages of 16 and 35. Most studies report that a higher number of women than men are affected, usually by a 3:1 ratio, although this ratio may be misleading. Many male patients in alcohol treatment facilities report that they started drinking to "medicate" themselves against their anxiety and panic symptoms. If this is true, then the actual sex ratio may be more equal, with many male alcoholics having hidden panic disorders. Despite numerous exceptions, male agoraphobics tend to succumb to phobic avoidance less than women do. The sex role expectations of men to leave the house and earn a living may place more social pressure on men to minimize phobic avoidance.

The health consequences of panic disorder and agoraphobia are similar to those of major depression. These patients have poor physical and emotional health, are at risk for the abuse of alcohol and other drugs, have increased risks of suicide, have impaired social and marital functioning, and have an increased use of health care services (Markowitz et al., 1989).

Although panic disorders are chronic, there may be periods of remission for no apparent reason and periods in which the symptoms are worse. Often the periods of remission are characterized by depression or free-floating anxiety.

There is some speculation that separation anxiety in children and dependent or avoidant personality features in adults predispose persons to the disorder, but these speculations do not have clear empirical support (Marks, 1987). A family history of panic disorder or depression increases the likelihood of developing the disorder. The initial panic attack usually occurs after a loss (e.g., death or divorce) or a major life change (e.g., birth of a child).

COMBINING PANIC DISORDER AND AGORAPHOBIA

The *DSM-III* separated agoraphobia into two groups: agoraphobia with panic attacks, and agoraphobia without panic attacks. A third category, panic disorder, was also created. The *DSM-III-*

R revised the *DSM-III* by classifying agoraphobia as a complication of the panic disorder. The *DSM-IV* follows the pattern established in *DSM-III-R*. Agoraphobia without panic attacks is extremely rare and is listed as agoraphobia without history of panic disorder (see Table 1, p. 3).

The reclassification of panic disorders and agoraphobia makes sense from a diagnostic and treatment planning viewpoint because panic disorder and agoraphobia appear to be the same disorder at different levels of intensity, and not separate diagnostic entities. The age of onset and the description of the panic attacks of the two categories are identical. Furthermore, agoraphobic patients almost always claim that the panic preceded the phobic avoidance. Both panic disorder patients and agoraphobic patients typically develop "spontaneous" panic attacks in response to infusion of sodium lactate (an artificial means of inducing panic attacks), whereas persons without a history of panic attacks seldom show such a response (Sheehan, 1984).

Turner, S. L. Williams, et al. (1986) found that panic disorder patients were highly similar to agoraphobic patients in diagnostic features. They differed, however, in severity and number of complications. Agoraphobic patients, by definition, demonstrated more extensive phobic avoidance. Also, they were more interpersonally sensitive, were more prone to alcohol abuse, experienced fewer periods of spontaneous remission, and described more symptoms occurring during the panic attacks. In summary, agoraphobic patients appeared to have a more chronic or more severe form of panic disorder.

Although some persons do not meet the *DSM-III-R* and *DSM-IV* criteria for panic disorder because their panic attacks are not sufficiently frequent, they experience the same effect as those whose attacks can be diagnosed as panic disorder. That is, fear of an attack keeps these patients close to safe places, and they require the same treatment as diagnosable panic disorder patients.

MEDICAL SCREENING
OF PANIC ATTACK PATIENTS

A small minority of panic disorder patients have medical conditions that mimic panic attacks. Although not recognized within the *DSM-III-R*, some writers have called this the "organic anxiety disorder." The *DSM-IV* has established two new categories called "anxiety disorder due to a general medical condition" and "substance-induced anxiety disorder" to better account for anxiety problems due to medical or organic conditions. The physical symptoms of panic often lead these patients to believe they have a physical disorder, and most patients presenting for treatment of anxiety disorders have already had numerous physical examinations and medical tests before seeking mental health treatment. Patients who come directly for mental health treatment for panic attacks without a physical screening should receive a medical evaluation before or during early phases of treatment. The medical examination should include a thyroid evaluation because thyroid disorders may mimic panic attacks.

The psychotherapist should request a medical reevaluation in two situations. First, patients should be reexamined if they have atypical symptoms such as clouding of consciousness, loss of intellectual functioning, fainting, strong feelings of derealization followed by aggression or verbal hostility, the onset of the panic that coincides with a specific physical problem, age of onset before 16 or after 40, and lack of positive family history for panic disorder, depression, or anxiety. Second, patients should receive a medical reexamination if they fail to respond to standard psychological or pharmacological treatments.

The most common organic sources of anxiety include overuse of caffeine and withdrawal from drugs (including over-the-counter nonprescription drugs and illicit drugs, such as marijuana or cocaine) and alcohol. Caffeine commonly causes or exacerbates anxiety and panic disorders, and people vary substantially in their tolerance. Although some can consume large quantities of caffeine with no ill effects, others react to the amount in one or two cups of coffee, tea, or other sources. For some patients the moderate use of caffeine may counter the antianxiety effects of prescription medication or relaxation exercises. Abrupt discontinuation of large amounts of caffeine can cause withdrawal symptoms including headaches, tachycardia, agitation, or panic attacks. Many panic disorder patients have discontinued caffeine intake on their own because they realized it increased their anxiety and frequency of panic attacks. Other patients may resist giving up caffeine because the withdrawal includes anxiety symptoms.

COEXISTING OR COMPLICATING DISORDERS

The diagnosis and treatment planning for panic disorders and agoraphobia can be difficult. Some clinicians distinguish between simple and complex agoraphobia. Simple agoraphobic patients only have panic attacks and phobic avoidance without other psychological problems. Complex agoraphobic patients have a wide range of other psychological problems such as marital problems, major depression, and avoidant or dependent features.

Panic and Personality Disorders. Clinicians have noticed unique personality features among some persons who have panic disorder, leading to their use of such phrases as "the agoraphobic personality." Although various authors have used that term loosely and inconsistently, it does reflect the informal observation that some personality traits commonly appear among persons with panic disorders.

Recently more systematic research has focused on the relationship of panic disorders to Axis II disorders. Although it is important to understand the relationship of anxiety disorders to personality disorders for theoretical reasons, this monograph will focus only on the treatment implications. The presence of a personality disorder may influence the course and outcome of treatment and may help clarify apparently confusing and complicated symptom presentations (Gorton & Akhtar, 1990; D. Stein, Hollander, & Skodol, 1993).

The research data on the co-morbidity of personality disorders of patients with panic disorders has led to similar results despite a wide diversity of instruments used to measure personality disorders. Researchers have consistently found a high proportion of patients with Cluster II (dramatic) or Cluster III (avoidant/dependent) personality disorders, and many more patients had sub-threshold scores for those disorders (Friedman, Shear, & Frances, 1987; M. Green & Curtis, 1988; Klass, DiNardo, & Barlow, 1989; Mauri et al., 1992; Mavissakalian & Hamann, 1986; Mavissakalian, Hamann, & B. Jones, 1990; Pollack et al., 1992; Reich, 1986). Fewer patients had a Cluster I (odd/eccentric) diagnosis or symptoms. Table 5 (p. 35) contains the most commonly endorsed items in the Mavissakalian and Hamann (1987) study.

TABLE 5: COMMONLY ENDORSED CHARACTERISTICS AMONG AGORAPHOBICS

CHARACTERISTIC	PERSONALITY DISORDER	PERCENT ENDORSED
Desire for Affection	Avoidant	94%
Low Self-Esteem	Avoidant	70%
Indirect Resistance	Passive-Aggressive	64%
Hypersensitivity to Rejection	Avoidant	64%
Affective Instability	Borderline	64%
Hypersensitivity	Paranoid	61%
Lacks Self-Confidence	Dependent	61%
Intolerance of Being Alone	Borderline	48%
Social Withdrawal	Avoidant	39%
Unwilling to Enter Relationships	Avoidant	36%
Feeling Empty or Bored	Borderline	33%

Note: Using data from Mavissakalian and Hamann, 1987.

Personality disorders were more likely to occur in patients with extensive phobic avoidance (Friedman et al., 1987). Mavissakalian and Hamann (1987) found that patients with more personality disorder traits had a more severe symptom pattern, suggesting a covariation between symptom severity and the presence of personality disorders. Klass et al. (1989) suggested that anxiety patients with coexisting personality disorders were more likely to have a secondary diagnosis of dysthymia and a past diagnosis of major depression. Pollack et al. (1992) found the same relationship between depression and coexisting personality disorders.

They also found that personality disorder patients were more likely to have other anxiety disorders and a more chronic course of their panic disorder. The subgroup of panic disorder/agoraphobic patients with personality disorders tended to respond poorer to pharmacological treatment (M. Green & Curtis, 1988; Mavissakalian & Hamann, 1987).

The direction of causality between personality disorders and agoraphobic symptoms is not clear. It is not known if panic and agoraphobic symptoms predispose persons to develop personality disorders, or if the personality disorders and panic symptoms are caused by a similar underlying vulnerability.

Major depression is also a common complication of panic disorder and agoraphobia. Although rates of depression vary slightly from study to study, about half of agoraphobic patients display significant depressive symptoms at the start of treatment. The psychotherapist needs to distinguish major depression from the demoralization likely to accompany any severe psychiatric or medical disorder; the withdrawal and social isolation caused by the agoraphobia may create loneliness and demoralization. Patients often are so preoccupied with the panic attacks that they do not recognize the vegetative symptoms of depression as such and need to be asked about them directly or given the BDI, MMPI, or MCMI to ascertain whether they are present. A distinction also needs to be made between depression with panic attacks and panic disorder with depression. Patients with severe major depression commonly have panic attacks. The use of antidepressants may be indicated in cases of coexisting panic and major depression because the antidepressants can remedy both the depression and the panic.

The relationship between panic disorder and marital difficulties is controversial. Older theories held that agoraphobics had marital problems more often than nonagoraphobics - that the marital situation either created the panic disorder or kept the panic disorder patient dependent, and that marital therapy was needed. It also has been hypothesized that treating the agoraphobic may harm the marital relationship and that spouses (especially husbands) may sabotage the therapy program or become depressed themselves as partners become more assertive and less dependent. Recent studies, however, suggest that this is not necessarily typical. Although some panic disorder patients have poor marriages, and some husbands have an apparent codependency on their wives and resist change, most will support treatment (Barlow & Waddell, 1985). Treatment plans that incorporate spouses have become popular and have given therapists an opportunity to monitor marital relationships.

TREATMENTS FOR PANIC DISORDERS AND AGORAPHOBIA

Few disorders require as much treatment flexibility and variation as panic disorders. Currently, two main models of treatment selection which have merit, the behavioral and the pharmacological, are being promoted. Of course, neither is a pure model. Many behavior therapists encourage their patients to use benzodiazepines in conjunction with behavior therapy, and pharmacotherapists often use behavioral techniques as an adjunct to medication. The initial treatment choice depends on the preferences of the patient and the therapist and the existence of concurrent psychiatric problems.

Because neither medication nor behavior therapy alone will succeed with all panic disorder patients, psychotherapists should consider both approaches in cases of incomplete response. It is best to inform patients at the onset about different treatment options because some will have strong, preconceived biases about certain treatments. Some may insist upon medication and have no desire to participate in a behavioral program involving exposure to the feared situation or panic, whereas others may refuse to take medications under any circumstances. Most patients, however, are open to considering treatment options. Panic patients generally have endured so many years of distress without relief from symptoms that they are relieved to find a therapist who can understand the disorder and discuss treatment options.

We recommend starting treatment with a behavioral approach because it has a lower drop-out rate and better outcome than the pharmacological approach (Michelson & Marchione, 1991). Also, clinical evidence suggests that it is easier to shift from a behavioral approach to a pharmacological approach than vice versa. Once relief from panic has been achieved by taking medication, these patients lose tolerance for the panic attacks that are an inevitable part of behavior therapy. Moreover, the skills learned in behavior therapy (such as graduated exposure and relaxation) are transferable to the medication program. We would, however, recommend a pharmacological approach first if the patient strongly preferred that modality, or if the patient evidenced concurrent severe major depression.

Core Approaches. Whatever the initial approach, we recommend starting treatment with an educational program and an assessment of the degree of disability. First, the psychotherapist should educate the patient about the nature of panic disorder. Typically patients are demoralized by the disorder and may have a great deal of self-blame. The educational program reduces self-blame by explaining that the panic attacks have a discernible basis, and that patients and their previous physicians have understandably not been able to identify or diagnose the attacks because of the bewildering array of symptoms that often present as panic disorder. In addition, the educational program should explain the possible treatment procedures. The procedures and outcome data concerning the various treatment options (behavioral and pharmacological) must be described accurately.

The educational program can be accomplished through bibliotherapy, discussions with the patient, questions and answers, contact with other panic disorder patients, and educational tapes. Panic disorder patients are greatly relieved to learn that they are not crazy or malingerers, and that treatments are available for their disorder. Knapp and VandeCreek (1988) have recommended various valuable books. For example, *Agoraphobia: A Clinical and Personal Account* (Clarke & Wardman, 1985), written by a former phobic, provides a very personalized description of the symptoms and treatment. Several excellent books have also been written by therapists, including *More Hope and Help for Your Nerves* (Weekes, 1984), *Fighting Fear* (Neuman, 1985), *Your Phobia* (Zane & Milt, 1984), and *Living with Fear* (Marks, 1978).

Concurrent with the education of the patient, the psychotherapist can assess the degree of the patient's disability in daily living. This will help to establish a baseline of avoidance behaviors and make it possible to monitor progress throughout treatment.

Several questionnaires can aid in determining the degree of debilitation and the optimal procedures for starting treatment. For example, the Agoraphobic Cognitions Questionnaire includes items pertaining to catastrophic thoughts about the results of panic, and the Body Sensations Questionnaire asks about physical sensations associated with anxiety (Chambless et al., 1984). The Mobility Inventory provides an index of fear of travel (Chambless et al., 1985). Finally, the Fear Questionnaire (FQ) is a brief, 23-item scale for assessing social phobia or agoraphobia (Marks & Matthews, 1979). We have included copies of these measures in the "Appendices" section (pp. 77-90). Simple behavioral diaries can supplement the various questionnaires by having patients identify apparent precipitants to their panic attack. Of course all of these assessment tools can be readministered to assess progress in therapy.

Behavioral Models. In our view, behavioral treatment programs using graduated exposure procedures have been most successful with panic disorder patients. Other treatment programs using indirect exposure (systematic desensitization, imaginal flooding), cognitive modification, or strictly verbal psychotherapies have a much lower success rate. Of course, indirect exposure and cognitive modification procedures can be added to enhance the effectiveness of direct exposure.

Several authors have described the direct exposure methods in detail (Barlow & Waddell, 1985; Beck & Emery, 1985; Weekes, 1984; Zane & Milt, 1984). These programs all require exposure to the feared panic attacks. Patients can substantially reduce or eliminate panic attacks when they learn to identify their precursors through monitoring their thoughts and mental images. Outcome studies have shown that about 70% of the patients with graduated exposure programs show clinically significant improvement.

Behavioral treatment programs are commonly combined with adjunctive treatments such as spousal involvement or paradoxical intention. Spouses can aid therapy by becoming more knowledgeable about the phobia and by accompanying the patient on outings. Involving the spouse may also strengthen the marriage. Paradoxical intention is also useful for controlling the heightened sense of anticipatory anxiety and should be explained honestly and openly without any effort to trick the patient.

Often when the graduated exposure is successful, patients still feel some residual anxiety similar to a mild generalized anxiety disorder state. They do not report panic attacks but still feel high physiological arousal. In these situations, psychotherapists need to determine the origin of the background anxiety. In some situations, anticipatory anxiety or fear of another panic attack may cause this anxiety. In other situations it may be due to a generalized worry about life situations in general.

If fear of future panic attacks causes the background anxiety, then psychotherapists need to determine if the patient continues to have minor or monosymptomatic panic attacks. If so, more work needs to be done to control these attacks. If the patient is not having panic attacks but still fears them, the therapist needs to explain how the fear of the panic attacks developed over many years and will dissipate with time as the patient has more and more success in subverting the attacks and achieving mobility.

If a generalized fear of a number of situations causes the background anxiety, then the psychotherapist may need to treat the patient as a generalized anxiety disorder (GAD) patient (see the section entitled "Generalized Anxiety Disorder," pp. 65-69). In either case, these patients may benefit from relaxation procedures, cognitive procedures to identify anxiety-invoking thoughts, or benzodiazepines to reduce the background anxiety. Finally, many patients with panic disorders have coexisting psychological problems that also need attention.

Only since the publication of *DSM-III-R* has the issue of comorbidity received the attention it deserves. However, data do not yet exist to guide practitioners on selecting the optimal treatment protocols for most patients with coexisting disorders (Brown & Barlow, 1992). Once again, practitioners must rely on theoretical or clinical guidance for combining treatment techniques for patients with more than one disorder.

Pharmacological Approaches. Several medications are useful for the treatment of panic disorders (Sheehan, 1984). Although the exact pharmacological mechanisms are not known, the medications appear to raise the threshold for the development of panic attacks. Many patients report that medication significantly reduces or eliminates spontaneous panic attacks, although these patients may still experience panic in crisis situations. Interestingly, successful responders to medication no longer respond to sodium lactate infusion by experiencing a panic attack.

The pharmacotherapist has several medications from which to choose. Tricyclic antidepressants (TCAs) have proven successful in reducing panic attacks. Monoamine oxidase inhibitors (MAOIs) have a slightly higher success rate but require strict dietary precautions (Sheehan, 1984). Recently, alprazolam (Xanax) also has been found to reduce panic attacks. Of the patients who complete pharmacological treatments, 50% show substantial improvement and another 30% show moderate improvement. However, the rest drop out of treatment because of their inability or unwillingness to tolerate side-effects. Another 33% will refuse even to try a pharmacological treatment. Consequently, only about 50% of patients presenting for treatment of panic disorders will benefit from medications.

The pharmacotherapist needs to consider several factors in choosing between antidepressants and alprazolam to suppress panic attacks. Alprazolam works faster in controlling panic attacks, but does not have as much effect on depression as the other drugs. The discontinuation of alprazolam almost always leads to a sudden recurrence of the panic attacks and to withdrawal symptoms. Antidepressants, however, have a lower rate of relapse. Goldstein (1986) suggested maximizing the positive qualities of both medications by starting the patient on alprazolam to suppress panic attacks rapidly, and then gradually switching to antidepressants which have a more broad-based positive impact. Patients who fail to respond to the tricyclic antidepressants can be switched to MAOIs, which are generally more potent in addressing symptoms than the TCAs.

As noted previously, patients with coexisting personality disorders do not respond as well to treatment as patients without these disorders.

According to Sheehan (1984), the use of medications to suppress panic attacks does not eliminate the need for behavior therapy. Rather, Sheehan follows a two-step procedure in which the medication reduces the panic attacks followed by behavior therapy (through desensitization or graduated exposure) to reduce the phobic avoidance.

A CASE VIGNETTE

Marvin is a 36-year-old unemployed laborer referred to a mental health clinic by his family doctor. He complained of attacks of numbness in his arms, dizziness, and buzzing in his ears. He had not experienced any of these attacks in the last month, but he was afraid they would occur again. He described anticipatory anxiety at work and nervousness around people in general. He reported being shy as a child and he apparently showed separation anxiety when he started school. A family doctor had prescribed Centrax three times a day, but Marvin complained that it did not stop his "fits." The panic attacks started when he separated from his wife 4 years ago, and he had not held steady employment since then. He said that he was afraid to return to work until he "got his strength back." The Life History Questionnaire showed a long pattern of isolation and extreme dependency upon his ex-wife and parents. Immediate family members were his only consistent source of social contact. He often drank alcohol to the point of intoxication. When drinking, he lost his social inhibitions and occasionally tried to develop a relationship with a woman at a bar. He had few friends, lived with his parents, and frequently talked about how much he missed his ex-wife. He felt nervous in shopping malls or other public places even when accompanied by his mother or other family members.

Diagnosis and Treatment Recommendations

Diagnosis. Axis I: Panic Disorder Without Agoraphobia
Axis II: Avoidant Personality Disorder

Treatment Plan. This case has all the markings of panic disorder with agoraphobia, but it does not meet that criterion technically because the panic attacks have not occurred in the last month. From a treatment point of view, however, Marvin can be considered to have a panic disorder.

The psychotherapist needs to assess several more of Marvin's characteristics, especially those related to a likely longstanding avoidant personality disorder. Although not mentioned in the vignette, Marvin is probably highly vulnerable to depression, which the BDI should reveal. Further assessment should clarify the nature of the patient's cognitive, physiological, and social skills functioning, because these areas are generally problematic in social phobia.

Other possible starting points for treatment depend on the results of further assessment. Social skills training most likely would be indicated for a patient manifesting avoidant personality disorder. The treatment of his or her panic disorder would be the same as for any panic disorder patient.

Therapists may find several self-report measures to be helpful in understanding the patient's anxiety disorder. Several inventories are reproduced in the "Appendices" section (pp. 77-90).

OBSESSIVE-COMPULSIVE DISORDERS

Robert is a 25-year-old married postal employee. He comes from a strict religious family and is an active member in his local church. He recently became the father of a healthy baby girl. For the past several months he has been bothered by intrusive thoughts and images of harming his wife and baby. He has had clear mental pictures of strangling his wife and throwing their baby into their wood-burning stove. These images have created a great deal of anxiety, but he has not been able to stop them. He has never acted violently toward anyone and appears to be an active and loving father.

Robert has an obsessive-compulsive disorder (OCD). The *DSM-IV* defines obsessions as ("persistent ideas, thoughts, impulses, or images that are experienced as intrusive and inappropriate and that cause marked anxiety or distress"/(American Psychiatric Association, 1994, p. 418). The *DSM-IV* defines compulsions as:

repetitive behaviors (e.g., hand washing, ordering, check-ing) or mental acts (e.g., praying, counting, repeating words silently) the goal of which is to prevent or reduce anxiety or distress, not to provide pleasure or gratifica-tion. In most cases, the person feels driven to perform the compulsion to reduce the distress that accompanies an obsession or to prevent some dreaded event or situation. (p. 418)

Obsessions are usually thoughts and compulsions are usually behaviors. However, the *DSM-IV* (American Psychiatric Associa-tion, 1994) properly notes that ultimately obsessions and compul-sions should be classified according to their functions. Obses-sions have no discernible end point and increase anxiety, while compulsions have an end point and are chosen to reduce anxiety. Compulsions may sometimes be cognitive, such as the use of prayers, mantras, or reciting numbers with the intent to ward off unwanted events, or be passive and include avoiding places of contamination.

Obsessions and compulsions are significant sources of dis-tress to the individual and interfere with social functioning. His-torically OCD was believed to be rare; now it is known that it has a lifetime prevalence of 2.5% (Rasmussen & Eisen, 1992). The reasons for the previous underestimation of the prevalence are that many patients were ashamed and secretive about the disorder, or psychotherapists failed to ask basic screening questions for OCD in their routine mental examinations. Asking a few basic questions, such as "Do you sometimes wash your hands over and over?" or "Do you feel a need to check things over and over again?" or "Do you have intrusive and unwanted thoughts that you would like to get rid of?" may identify patients with OCD who otherwise would not describe these symptoms.

Obsessive-compulsive disorders appear with equal frequency in men and women. These disorders have a bimodal age of onset, commonly appearing in early adolescence or the late 20s. Onset often follows a major life event such as the birth of a child, the start of a new job, or a move to a new home. Onset beyond the age of 35 is rare and, in such cases, a neurological evaluation is advisable to rule out possible organic causes. Before the age of

35, medical and neurological evaluations are almost always negative (Jenike, 1983).

DIFFERENTIAL DIAGNOSIS

The hierarchal rules apply to OCD disorders. The OCD diagnosis cannot be made if another psychiatric disorder such as Tourette's, schizophrenia, or major depression causes the obsessions or compulsions.

Obsessions and compulsions often occur in other *DSM-III-R* and *DSM-IV* diagnoses and it is important to distinguish OCD from other major disorders. Sometimes the line between obsessions and schizophrenia is hard to draw. The general rule of thumb is that schizophrenia involves ego-syntonic thoughts and impulses. That is, the person with schizophrenia views them as realistic. This distinction is helpful most of the time, although in some situations it is hard to differentiate an overvalued idea of an OCD patient from a delusion of a schizophrenia patient.

Compulsions or stereotypic movements sometimes occur within Tourette's syndrome or with organic brain syndrome (OBS) patients. In OBS patients the repetitive behaviors are caused by an inability to vary performance and are not used to reduce anxiety. In Tourette's they are due to a neurological condition, serve no purpose, and are not used to reduce anxiety.

Some researchers have opined that Tourette's, anorexia nervosa, bulimia, dysmorphophobia, and some forms of compulsive gambling or sexual fetishes fall within an OCD spectrum of disorders. We will not review the literature on this topic. However, we will note that, at this time, it is prudent to diagnose them as separate disorders and treat them accordingly. Although some of these disorders, such as Tourette's and dysmorphophobia, have a higher co-morbidity with OCD, research has not developed a unified treatment strategy for these disorders or identified treatment value in considering them as variants of OCD.

The lifetime risk of having OCD plus an associated anxiety disorder is high. Many OCD patients report specific or social phobias, panic disorders, agoraphobia, or motor tics. However, major depression is the most common co-morbid disorder found with OCD.

OCD and Depression. The distinction between depression and obsessions may be difficult to establish. At times obsessions result from depression and lift as the depression is treated; at other times the depression follows the OCD disorder. The rule is to look for the sequence in symptom development. Depression that follows the onset of OCD may be more properly characterized as demoralization than depression. OCD symptoms alone are likely to produce despair, hopelessness, and self-reproach. In fact, Turner, McCann, et al. (1986) and Barlow et al. (1986) found the average OCD patient to have Beck Depression Inventory scores high enough to qualify as major depression (see Table 3, p. 8), but these symptoms do not necessarily warrant a diagnosis of depression. Vegetative symptoms of depression most commonly distinguish primary depression from demoralization. For patients with vegetative symptoms or a depression that was present before the OCD, it is necessary to treat the depression first through either psychotherapy or medication before working on the obsessions and compulsions (Steketee & Foa, 1985).

OCD and Personality Disorders. The research on OCD and personality disorders has been complicated by very different methodologies in assessing personality disorders. Nevertheless, it does appear that many patients with OCD have coexisting personality disorders, especially obsessive-compulsive personality disorder or schizotypal personality disorder. A finding of a relationship between OCD and other personality disorders has less support.

Early theorists speculated that OCD was a variant of obsessive-compulsive personality disorder. Later research has not supported this concept. It is true that patients with obsessive-compulsive personality disorder have an almost ritualistic preoccupation with details. But the compulsions in OCD patients are ego-syntonic and have no anxiety-reducing features. Although many OCD patients have compulsive traits or obsessive-compulsive personality disorders, the majority of OCD patients do not meet the criteria for obsessive-compulsive personality disorder. In fact, other personality disorders are as common with OCD as the obsessive-compulsive personality disorder (Pfohl & Blum, 1991).

Stanley, Turner, and Borden (1989) and Jenike et al. (1986) have found that a significant minority of OCD patients had schizotypical personality disorders. They frequently had odd speech, inadequate social support, suspiciousness, hypersensitivity, and social isolation. They were also characterized by magical thinking, ideas of reference, and depersonalization. Unless the schizotypal features are addressed, these persons will have a poor response to standard treatments for OCD. Jenike et al. (1986) recommended that such patients participate in structured activities such as day treatment programs which address this personality disorder. This finding of a significant coexistence of OCD and schizotypal personality disorder may have been responsible for the false belief that OCD was a precursor of schizophrenia.

Other researchers have found "dramatic" personality disorders (especially histrionic and borderline) or "avoidant" personality disorders (avoidant, dependent) common among OCD patients (Mavissakalian et al., 1990). Nevertheless, their findings suggest that some OCD patients may have interpersonal difficulties that may complicate the psychotherapist-patient relationship.

SUBTYPES OF OBSESSIVE-COMPULSIVE DISORDERS

The subtypes of OCD require different kinds of treatment. The most common subtype presents obsessions followed by compulsions such as a compulsion to clean or to avoid contamination from dirt or other noxious substances. Another OCD subtype includes those who experience obsessions without compulsions. This subgroup often describes obsessions with violating important social norms such as acting aggressively or sexually. A final rare form of OCD is called primary obsessional slowness. Patients with this disorder act as if life were in slow motion and take many hours to perform simple routine life skills such as shaving or dressing.

The Maudsley Obsessional-Compulsive (MOC) Inventory (Hodgson & Rachman, 1977) may help psychotherapists to assess the existence and extent of different obsessive-compulsive complaints. This inventory yields information about observable rituals of cleaning, checking, slowness, and doubting. The inventory is quick to administer (10 to 15 minutes) and easy to score (30 items in a true-false format), controls for an acquiescent response set, and includes only items that differentiate obsessional from nonobsessional neurotics. A copy of the MOC is reprinted in the "Appendices" section (pp. 77-90). A total score and subscale scores for cleaning, checking, slowness, and doubting are obtained by totaling the number of questions that are answered in the obsessional direction. Table 6 (below) compares mean number of responses on the MOC by obsessionals and nonobsessional neurotics.

TREATMENTS FOR OBSESSIVE-COMPULSIVE DISORDERS

For many years the treatment of OCD was very difficult and characterized by low success rates. Even these low success rates were probably exaggerated because they included obsessive-compulsive personality disorders within the samples of OCD patients. Now advances in behavioral and pharmacological treatments have led to new hope for these patients.

TABLE 6: DATA FOR OBSESSIONAL AND NONOBSESSIONAL NEUROTIC INDIVIDUALS*

	OBSESSIONALS ($N = 100$)		NEUROTICS ($N = 50$)	
	Mean	Standard Deviation	Mean	Standard Deviation
Total	18.86	4.92	9.27	5.43
Checking	6.10	2.21	2.84	2.29
Cleaning	5.55	3.04	2.38	1.97
Slowness	3.63	1.93	2.27	1.09
Doubting	5.39	1.60	3.69	1.99

*Note: From "Obsessional Compulsive Complaints" by R. J. Hodgson and S. Rachman, 1977, *Behaviour Research and Therapy, 15,* pp. 389-395. Copyright © 1977 by the Pergamon Journals, Ltd. Reprinted with permission.

Obsessions With Compulsions. The optimal treatments for OCD vary according to the subtype of the disorder and the presence of coexisting disorders. Response prevention is the optimal treatment for obsessions followed by compulsions. Typically these patients have cleaning compulsions (and obsessions of dirt or filth) or checking compulsions (and obsessional doubt or guilt). Briefly, response prevention means exposing the patient for prolonged periods (45 minutes to 2 hours) to situations that produce anxiety. Often the anxiety can be heightened by having the patient engage in the most feared activities, for example, touching a "contaminated" object. In the past, these patients would avoid the contaminated object or use rituals such as cleaning dirt or checking stoves to reduce their anxiety. In response prevention, however, they are not permitted to engage in these anxiety-avoiding or anxiety-reducing activities. Instead, they are exposed to the very stimuli that upsets them the most. Patients stay in the situation until their anxiety dissipates, and the exposure is graded so that mildly upsetting situations will precede the most upsetting ones. Leaving the situation before the anxiety decreases is countertherapeutic and strengthens rather than weakens the relationship between anxiety and avoidance. Often the patient needs 10 to 20 sessions before treatment is completed (Steketee & Foa, 1985).

Outcome studies from a variety of treatment centers have found success rates with response prevention of about 75% for patients who comply with treatment. Follow-up studies show that the treatment effects last, although some patients may require booster sessions. The outcome for response prevention is substantially higher than for any other treatment program for obsessive-compulsive disorders (Steketee & Foa, 1985). The relapse rate for successful completers of behavior therapy is far less than that found in patients who discontinue medications.

Despite the positive response of behavior therapy, researchers have identified several patient factors that limit its effectiveness. As noted previously, if severe depression coexists with the OCD, the medication or psychotherapy for the depression is indicated before beginning the response prevention program.

Other factors that limit the effectiveness of behavior therapy include the failure to comply with treatment through the use of covert mental rituals or with drop-outs due to the discomfort found in the exposure to the feared stimuli. The assessment of OCD disorders requires the identification of the obsessions (anxiety-inducing thoughts or acts) and compulsions (anxiety-reducing thoughts or acts). If response prevention is to be successful, then the anxiety-reducing thoughts must be blocked, requiring the psychotherapist to identify all compulsions, even cognitive compulsions. Although most compulsions are overt behavioral acts, others may be cognitive such as repeating a prayer, mantra, or ritualistic saying. The patient must block these cognitive compulsions through distraction or thought stopping in order for response prevention to have its maximum success.

Another area of assessment relevant to the treatment of obsessions with compulsions includes the identification of active and passive forms of avoidance. Active avoidance is easily identifiable, such as the cleaning compulsive who cleans up incessantly until the house is completely in order. Passive avoidance is less easy to detect. Examples include persons who sit on the edge of the chair so as not to pick up excessive dirt from the chair, who open the door with the tips of their fingers to avoid touching dirt, or who avoid going certain places associated with filth. A successful response prevention program must circumvent passive avoidance as well as the obvious active avoidance.

Finally, response prevention has not had good success with a minority of obsessive-compulsives with "overvalued ideas." These patients adhere with rigidity to certain illogical ideas, assigning high probabilities to feared consequences. Patients, for example, may insist that they have Autoimmune Deficiency Syndrome (AIDS), and seek repeated blood tests for AIDS, all of which prove negative. Such persistent thoughts must be altered before significant improvement can be made (Steketee & Foa, 1985). In the absence of fixed ideas, the success rate exceeds 75%.

The distinction between schizophrenic delusions and obsessional, overvalued ideas may be difficult to make. Although typically schizophrenia and OCD are clearly distinct, "overvalued ideas" represents a gray area in which the distinction between the two becomes blurred. In OCD these overvalued ideas may impede behavior therapy, but psychotic decompensation is rare.

We recommend that behavior therapy be the treatment of choice of persons with obsessions with compulsions. However, for persons who have contraindications for behavior therapy, medications that involve serotonin uptake inhibitors have been proven effective (see discussion below).

Obsessions Without Compulsions. Obsessions without compulsions are harder to treat with psychotherapy. The psychotherapist has several treatment options with lower rates of success (about 50% or less) than response prevention. The treatment options we recommend include paradoxical techniques or assertiveness training. The latter may be applicable when obsessions are of hurting other people, and it is assumed that aggression/assertiveness issues predominate.

Tricyclic antidepressants and monoamine oxidase inhibitors have had some modest success with this group. Several case reports have demonstrated dramatic improvements in response to tricyclic antidepressant medications. It is debatable whether these drugs have an antiobsessional property distinct from their antidepressant effects.

No outcome study has yet directly compared tricyclics to the various behavior therapy techniques in a group of obsessional patients. Both, however, have had some occasional successes. The responsible psychotherapist can start the nondepressed obsessional patient with either the behavioral or tricyclic approach, but remain flexible to consider adjunctive treatments or to switch treatments if desired results are not forthcoming. Depressed obsessional patients should probably start with antidepressants. As noted previously, demoralization is distinct from primary depression. Other pharmacological treatments such as anxiolytic agents or neuroleptics have had little effect with OCD disorders.

On the other hand, some recent medications such as clomipramine (anafranil), fluoxetine hydrochloride (Prozac), and fluvoxamine have been demonstrated most effective with OCD, and appear to have distinct antiobsessional qualities. Results also suggest fewer side-effects than with the older antidepressants (Goodman, McDougle, & Price, 1992). Although the outcome is not clear on this issue, it may be prudent to combine behavior therapy with medications for some patients who are poor candidates for behavior therapy alone.

Primary Obsessional Slowness. A small minority of OCD patients have primary obsessional slowness (Rachman, 1974; Veale, 1993). Such patients may take hours to perform routine tasks such as brushing teeth, shaving, or dressing. The degree of impairment, not unexpectedly, can be severe and impair ability to hold a job or sustain a marriage.

Several case studies have suggested that prompting, shaping, and pacing are helpful for this group of patients (see, e.g., Rachman, 1974). However, long-term studies of these patients are lacking, and more investigation is needed before the effectiveness of behavioral techniques can be fully established (Veale, 1993).

A CASE VIGNETTE

Linda is a 36-year-old housewife whose house is immaculate. The sight of dirt being tracked into her house was enough to precipitate extreme anxiety and hours of furtive cleaning. She made her husband take showers in the basement and insisted that her children repeatedly clean their rooms. Although her husband had catered to her wishes most of the time, he was tiring of her excessive preoccupation with cleanliness. When he talked with her about becoming more relaxed about cleaning, she insisted that household dirt transmits dreaded diseases like leukemia, cancer, and AIDS. No amount of persuasion seemed to convince her otherwise.

Diagnosis and Treatment Recommendations

Diagnosis.   Axis I: Obsessive-Compulsive Disorder
             Axis II: No Information

Treatment Plan. Acquiring Linda's cooperation will be difficult because of her fixed belief that her concerns are legitimate. If she does agree to treatment, however, response prevention is recommended for obsessions followed by compulsions. Depression should be assessed through the BDI or other instruments. The presence of any significant amount of depression may suggest the use of antidepressant medications.

POST-TRAUMATIC STRESS DISORDER

Phillip is a 45-year-old Vietnam veteran who was awarded a Purple Heart. Although he is proud of his military service in Vietnam, he seldom talks about it. For the previous 3 months he has had nightmares about an incident involving the death of several Vietnamese children. He has never discussed this event with anyone since he separated from the military and appeared to have forgotten it completely. He has become increasingly irritable and emotionally distant from his wife, and vegetative symptoms of depression have emerged. He mentioned his nightmares after several months of therapy and after reading an article about Post-Traumatic Stress Disorder (PTSD). The nightmares started shortly after a car struck and injured his youngest son.

Phillip has post-traumatic stress disorder (PTSD). Although recent research has focused on emotionally disturbed Vietnam veterans, there is growing recognition that many types of catastrophes such as rape, crime victimization, torture, floods, or other natural disasters can cause PTSD. The essential feature of PTSD is that the syndrome develops out of a trauma that is "outside the range of usual human experience" (American Psychiatric Association, 1987, p. 247).

The characteristic symptoms include (a) persistent reexperiencing of the traumatic event through recurrent and intrusive recollections, startle responses to stimuli that symbolize or resemble the original trauma, *déjà vu* experiences, or nightmares; (b) persistent avoidance of stimuli related to the trauma through numbing of responsiveness; and (c) increased arousal resulting in symptoms such as difficulty sleeping, outbursts of anger, and hypervigilance.

The *DSM-III* provided a major advance in formally recognizing the sufferings of trauma survivors, which previously had been underestimated. The *DSM-I* had a diagnostic category called "gross stress reaction," but it specified that this reaction would dissipate quickly. The *DSM-II* also included a category for short-lived, trauma-induced symptoms called "transient situational disturbance." These previous diagnostic categories minimized the effects of the trauma and emphasized the preexisting difficulties of the individual. The category of PTSD first appeared in the *DSM-III*. The *DSM-III-R* diagnosis of PTSD requires that the triggering event be so stressful as to create a disturbance in virtually everyone. The *DSM-IV* (American Psychiatric Association, 1994) revised that portion of the PTSD definition to include witnessing the event occurring to oneself or others. Another option would include a sense of helplessness, intense fear, or horror in reaction to the event.

The *DSM-IV* has included a new category called "acute stress disorder" which includes persons with symptoms that occur within 1 month after exposure to a traumatic stressor and resolve within that 1-month period.

The optimal way to diagnose PTSD is through a detailed clinical interview, although some psychological tests may have supplemental value. The diagnostic interview should focus on the nature and severity of the stressor, the denial/intrusiveness continuum, and associated symptoms. Effective treatment requires identification of the unique social and psychological manifestations for the individual patient.

SEVERITY OF STRESSOR

Usually the likelihood of developing, and the severity of, PTSD varies directly with the severity of the event. Survivors of stressors that involved severe physical and psychological threat or damage have developed the most severe symptoms of PTSD. Persons who survived floods and fires, for example, were more likely to develop PTSD if they lost a loved one or if they had extreme property loss. Similarly, American prisoners of war (POWs) from World War II were more likely to develop psychiatric disorders if they were in Japanese prison camps as opposed to German prison camps which, on the whole, were less traumatizing.

On the other hand, the loss or trauma may be symbolic or subtle. The loss of family heirlooms, cherished trinkets, or photographs in a fire may, for example, be more stressful than the loss of many thousands of dollars. A rape victim who loses her virginity in the absence of other physical harm may suffer more of a trauma than an assault or accident victim with substantially more severe physical trauma. The threatened loss of a loved one may be sufficient to activate PTSD.

Nevertheless, trauma does not necessarily lead to PTSD. For some, the trauma may result in an uncomplicated depression, an adjustment disorder, or another psychological disturbance. For example, survivors of rape do not necessarily develop PTSD after their experiences, although those reporting rapes have twice the lifetime prevalence of psychopathology and 10 times the likelihood of attempting suicide as nonvictims. The reasons for the differential reaction to traumatic events is not clear, but may have to do with the degree of trauma experienced, its context, the psychological impact, and the social and coping resources of the individual.

DENIAL

An essential feature in determining whether PTSD develops is the denial/intrusiveness dimension. Under periods of extreme stress, victims may block out or deny traumatic experiences. Concentration camp survivors, rape victims, torture survivors, and combat veterans often avoid talking about their experiences - or at least the most upsetting experiences. Combat veterans may, for example, tell war stories in a casual manner. This may be misleading and give the impression that the war did not particularly bother them. In fact, however, many veterans talk around their upsetting experiences and refuse to mention the severe traumas and losses they experienced.

The denial and numbing can be so strong that friends, relatives, and even some unsuspecting psychotherapists do not recognize PTSD symptoms. This happened when American and German psychiatrists interviewed concentration camp survivors following World War II in order to evaluate their eligibility to receive disability benefits. Many psychiatrists initially pronounced them normal and free of psychiatric disability. The survivors, as part of the numbing process, denied any severe psychiatric problems or greatly minimized them. The unsophisticated psychiatrists did not know to probe or look for specific symptoms of the disorder and concluded that these survivors were mentally healthy (Krystal, 1968).

Similar experiences were found in the evaluation of the survivors of the Buffalo Creek flood in West Virginia. The survivors of the Buffalo Creek flood instituted a multimillion-dollar lawsuit against the owners of the dam that broke and flooded the valley. As part of the lawsuit, legal counsel hired mental health experts to assess the degree of psychological impairment.

Although the plaintiffs had financial incentives to exaggerate their symptoms, they did not. More experienced psychotherapists knew to look for PTSD symptoms, but were nonetheless impressed by the degree of denial and minimization which they found in the survivors (Titchener & Kapp, 1976).

INTRUSIVENESS

The counterpart of the numbing dimension is intrusive thoughts. This may occur as nightmares, or through relatively innocuous pictures or scenes that trigger *déjà vu* experiences or memories. Cases have been recorded wherein survivors were mistakenly identified as having schizophrenia because of the strength of the intrusive memories. For example, a woman walking down the streets of New York had a sudden feeling that she was back in the concentration camp. This, however, was not a schizophrenic hallucination, but an intrusive thought or memory caused by a triggering object in the environment (Krystal, 1968).

At times survivors may reenact elements of the trauma. Reenactments by combat veterans may take the form of aggressive behavior, and assaults on innocent bystanders have been reported.

Research with combat veterans suggests that the two predominant symptoms, denial and intrusiveness, tend to segregate according to specific forms of precipitating events. Veterans who only witnessed violence tended to have reexperiencing symptoms, and those participating in violence tended to have more denial symptoms. The research is insufficient to determine if this distinction applies to all forms of trauma.

The actual patient presentation of PTSD may represent a very wide range and variety of symptoms depending on the nature of the trauma, its social and psychological context, the culture of the survivor, and many other factors. Nevertheless, studies with various survivor groups have found enough similarities in the basic symptomatology to justify PTSD as a single entity which extends to a variety of survivor groups.

ACUTE OR DELAYED ONSET

Post-traumatic stress disorder (PTSD) can have either an acute or delayed onset. Acute PTSD occurs immediately or soon after the trauma. Delayed symptoms may appear several months or years after the trauma. The delayed phenomenon is well-documented although less frequent than acute PTSD. Usually a triggering event reminds the person of his or her vulnerability or loss (such as the preceding example of Phillip).

OTHER FEATURES OF PTSD

Reliable information on the prevalence, duration, sex ratio, and natural course of the disorder is lacking. Although anecdotal information is extensive, scientific research on PTSD is more limited. Anecdotal reports from a variety of sources such as American soldiers in World War II, survivors of assaults and rape, concentration camps, and the Hiroshima nuclear bombing all give evidence of an anxiety disorder meeting the criteria of the *DSM-III-R* and *DSM-IV*. Although greatly valued, these anecdotes do not contain information on the course of the disorder, and they lack standardized psychometric measures or uniform interviewing procedures.

These anecdotes, however, suggest that the disorder can fluctuate over time and become worse in the presence of certain triggering stimuli or during anniversary events. For example, humid weather may make a survivor of a Japanese POW camp think about those experiences, or the smell of a certain male antiperspirant deodorant may evoke memories in a survivor of a rape or assault.

Reliable information on the incidence of PTSD in the general population is lacking. Although it can be found in 5% to 20% of war veterans, no data are available on the presence of PTSD in other groups. Nevertheless, it is high among survivors of unusual situations such as concentration camps (Krystal, 1968), tortured political prisoners (Somnier & Genefke, 1986), survivors of violent crimes (Bard & Sangry, 1986), and survivors of natural catastrophes (Raphael, 1986). Women are more likely to report PTSD, but this may reflect their greater exposure to traumatic events. The age of onset depends on the age of the trauma.

Post-traumatic stress disorder can also occur in persons such as military medics, nurses, or rescue workers who are exposed to the carnage of war or catastrophe (Van Devanter & Morgan, 1984). Usually the likelihood of developing PTSD increases with exposure to human mutilation or corpses.

MODERATING FACTORS FOR PTSD

The study of PTSD has been characterized by intense discussion of the role of moderating factors in the development of PTSD. It is not understood why some persons develop PTSD in response to a trauma, but others do not. The discussion has been tainted by a fear that some researchers will return to a "blame the victim" attitude.

Regrettably, some of the early theories of trauma did focus too much on the preexisting personality of the victims and minimized the effect of the trauma. Recent theories implicate several biological and psychological factors in the etiology of PTSD. Evidence seems to suggest that PTSD develops out of a complex interaction between biological and psychological predispositions, the occurrence of stressful events, the development of anxiety in response to the stress, and the adequacy of coping strategies and social support (J. C. Jones & Barlow, 1990).

Studies of the effects of age, gender, or preexisting psychopathology have not led to consistent results. Nevertheless, there is some suggestion that survivors with active coping styles respond better to disasters (Gibbs, 1989).

Also, survivors with strong social support systems and early access to supportive persons are less likely to develop PTSD. The social support relationship is consistent with findings concerning the moderating effects of social support with most psychological disorders. The benefits of early access to supportive persons has given rise to rape trauma centers, mental health responses to natural disasters, debriefings for military personnel in combat, and other primary prevention efforts.

Ego-dystonic features tend to exacerbate the effects of the trauma. That is, persons who felt guilt or shame over what they did or failed to do have more severe PTSD. This occurs in concentration camp survivors who feel guilty because they did not resist, in combat veterans for violating codes against killing, in rape victims because they did not fight back aggressively enough, or in survivors of torture who revealed information under duress. Self-attributions of guilt are quite frequent, although survivors are usually too severe on themselves. Women who are assaulted physically in the course of a rape, for example, are less likely to develop PTSD than those who are "only" threatened with assault. It appears that the actual assault reduces the amount of guilt or second-guessing about fighting back and provides public evidence of resistance.

COEXISTING OR COMPLICATING DISORDERS

Often PTSD patients have symptoms that warrant other concurrent diagnoses. To date, it is not clear whether the common coexisting diagnoses vary as a consequence of the demographic or personality features of the survivor or the nature of the trauma. Survivors of rape, assaults, and natural catastrophes often have coexisting major depressions. It may be beneficial to inquire about the possibility of previous trauma through assault, natural catastrophe, or military experiences of patients presenting mixtures of anxiety, depression, or somatic preoccupation. Victims of violent crime also show a substantial increase in alcohol abuse after the crime occurred.

American Vietnam veterans often have secondary diagnoses of drug or alcohol abuse, antisocial personality disorders, or depression. Because American men predominately from middle to lower classes served in combat in Vietnam, it is not known if their background predisposed them toward antisocial personality disorder, if men with a predisposition to develop personality disorders were more likely to seek out combat experiences, or if the combat experiences led to the development of personality disorders.

Many veterans used alcohol to medicate themselves to dull memories, nightmares, and intrusive responses. The alcohol or drugs may create independent problems, however, in that they may lead to hallucinations during withdrawal which are similar to intrusive thoughts. It can be hard to determine the cause of such hallucinations. Also, sometimes alcohol withdrawal lowers the seizure threshold, and some severely impaired PTSD patients with alcoholism may have actual alcohol withdrawal-induced seizures.

In contrast, survivors of natural disasters, torture, concentration camps, and criminal assaults usually have depression as a co-existing disorder and are less likely to have drug abuse or personality disorders, although substance abuse will sometimes occur with these persons.

TREATMENT CHOICES

The treatment of PTSD is unique among psychiatric disorders and especially anxiety disorders because there are no controlled outcome studies with this disorder. There have been, for example, controlled studies with survivors of rape experiences, but their authors do not demonstrate that all victims who served as subjects met criteria for PTSD. Instead, the treatment groups may have been "contaminated" with persons with other diagnoses. In part, this is because the diagnosis was relatively new, appearing for the first time in the *DSM-III*. More importantly, PTSD survivors are often reluctant to participate in treatment programs or outcome studies. It is characteristic of this disorder that the survivors desire to minimize or deny the disability. Treatment studies have not incorporated appropriate experimental control groups, or were limited to case studies. Drop-out rates are often high in the uncontrolled studies.

Nonetheless, a number of case histories and uncontrolled studies provide suggestions on how to proceed with treatment. The treatments follow many different theoretical orientations including psychodynamic, behavioral, or biochemical interventions. Despite differences in these approaches, three themes emerge. First, successful treatments must involve some kind of confrontation or exposure to the trauma (Fairbanks & Nicholson, 1987). Second, the treatment must be tailored to the individual characteristics of the patient. Third, medication may be a useful adjunct to relieve some of the symptoms of PTSD, but is seldom sufficient by itself.

Exposure to Traumatic Memories. Successful treatments expose the survivor to some aspect of the traumatic memory. This may mean the very painful process of discussing or imagining an event that evokes high anxiety and fear.

Exposure should occur in the context of a trusting relationship with the psychotherapist. The patient should never be forced to confront the trauma. Instead, the patient should retain ultimate control over the presentation of the imagery or discussion of the trauma. Since lack of control is one of the characteristics of experiencing a trauma, it could aggravate the patient's condition to expose him or her to an uncontrolled reexperiencing of the trauma. Finally, exposure must be done carefully and with an effort to reduce the discomfort so the patient will not abandon treatment.

Group psychotherapy or other forms of social support very often help in the exposure or confrontational stage. Group psychotherapy for PTSD received attention when used with Vietnam veteran "rap" groups in New York City (Lifton, 1973) and was later extended to other survivors such as crime victims or rape victims. One of the benefits of the group treatment is that the patients have a welcome atmosphere of acceptance. Vietnam veterans fear censorship for their participation in a war that lacked uniform popular support, and rape victims fear that others will condemn them for failing to take precautions or fight back hard enough.

Education of family and friends about the nature of PTSD is almost always indicated, especially if they hold dysfunctional beliefs about the role of the victim or otherwise withhold social support. It is important that these persons understand that the patient's reactions may be normal, given the nature of the stressor experienced.

Behavioral approaches such as guided imagery, flooding, or systematic desensitization can help reduce the anxiety associated with certain triggering stimuli or thoughts. Care needs to be taken, however, to obtain the cooperation of the patient and to explain the procedures and their rationale thoroughly. Memory of the events are often so painful that patients will avoid overly confrontive treatments.

Eye Movement Desensitization and Reprocessing (EMDR) has had some very promising outcomes with PTSD (e.g., Marquis, 1991; F. Shapiro, 1989). According to this treatment, lateral eye movements (saccades) produce a rapid decrease in distress associated with dysfunctional thoughts or images. F. Shapiro (1993) has refined EMDR to include considerations of rapport, pacing, client expectations, support systems, and other clinical variables. However, the procedure requires considerable training and may not be appropriate for all patients. Furthermore, detailed outcome studies and more precise delineation of the treatment methods are needed before this procedure can be recommended as a treatment of choice (Herbert & Mueser, 1992). Nevertheless, the positive reports suggest that EMDR needs to be taken seriously as a potential treatment of PTSD.

Individual Adaptation. The treatment must be tailored to the unique needs of the individual. Some of the factors that need to be considered are the culture and age of the patient, the relationship of the assailant (if any) to the patient, the presence of any ego-dystonic features, and coexisting diagnoses.

For example, for reasons that are not understood, many Khmer survivors of the killing fields developed blindness in the absence of any biological explanation (Kinzie & Boehnlein, 1989). Such psychogenic blindness has not been observed in torture survivors from other cultures. Most likely it represents a unique Khmer cultural response.

Some patients with severe forms of PTSD may have social withdrawal to the point of schizoidlike behavior. Although some patients regain social skills after the symptoms of PTSD are addressed, others may need social skills training. This may be especially important in traumatized children who may develop a distrust of others and an inability to form intimate relationships. Whereas adult survivors have already established social skills, the trauma may delay the development of appropriate social skills in children.

The relationship to the aggressor may influence treatment, because an assault by an unknown person may have very different psychological implications from assault by a family member. Family relationship issues may need to be addressed.

Whether the trauma included ego-dystonic or ego-syntonic features is also relevant. A person involved in a successful relief operation after a natural disaster may have different self-interpretations than one who participated in combat. Restructuring of attributions may be indicated. One of the important functions of self-help groups is to let survivors know that others have experienced similar reactions, thus helping them to realize that their reactions and behaviors were normal or understandable under the circumstances.

The psychological implications of the trauma for the individual need to be considered as well. A trauma that involves sexual violations, such as rape or incest, may have psychological implications different from a trauma following a natural disaster.

Finally, the treatment must consider whether the patient has any coexisting diagnoses. As noted before, the existence of a substance abuse diagnosis may complicate the symptom picture and treatment outcome.

Medications. Some preliminary research suggests distinct biological markers for PTSD, although no unifying biological theory has been developed to guide pharmacological treatments. Recent experience with medications shows that they have some benefit, although they should seldom be used alone to treat PTSD.

The rule of thumb is to use medications to treat the symptoms. Vegetative symptoms of depression are treated with imipramine, and general anxiety with benzodiazepines. Imipramine has become especially popular in the treatment of PTSD, although medications need to be used in combination with psychotherapy. The belief is that any medication that can reduce the hyperarousal would be beneficial to the patient. However, pharmacotherapists need to be careful about using benzodiazepines in PTSD patients with coexisting substance abuse problems. Neuroleptics may be indicated for hallucinations or flashback episodes.

A CASE VIGNETTE

Carol, a 27-year-old single woman with a major complaint of anxiety, sought assistance from a mental health center. She insisted on talking with a female therapist. In the first interview she described a suicide attempt that took place during the last year. She reported experiencing sudden mood changes and excessive nervousness for no apparent reason. She had a poor appetite, she had a low level of energy, and she slept poorly at night. She had broken up with her boyfriend during the past year. Although she blamed him for the failure of the relationship, it appeared from her description that she had become hostile and uncompromising with him. Although her behavior had a hostile, suspicious, and almost paranoid quality, she could not stand to be alone, and she frequently sought out the company of others to avoid the anxiety she felt when alone. During the second interview the psychotherapist learned that Carol had been raped about 1 year earlier. Her functioning before that time had been good. After the rape she developed a startle response to environmental cues that reminded her of the rape experience. She became afraid to be alone. Sex began to disgust her, and she terminated her relationship with her boyfriend (against his wishes). The very topic of rape upset her tremendously, and she seldom mentioned the experience to anyone. She blamed herself for not struggling more with her assailant. Her sleep was interrupted by frightening dreams to the point that she was afraid to go to sleep.

Diagnosis and Treatment Recommendations

Diagnosis.   Axis I: Post-Traumatic Stress Disorder
                         Major Depression
              Axis II: No diagnosis

Treatment Plan. The treatment should be implemented slowly and carefully so as not to frighten her. Given her past experience, it is reasonable to respect her preference for a female psychotherapist. Antidepressants may help relieve the vegetative depressive symptoms. Gradually the psychotherapist and patient may be able to identify the cues to her startle response and institute systematic desensitization or related strategies. The psychotherapist will allow her to talk about her experiences for the first time. One of the goals is to reduce her sense of self-blame. Eliciting the help of family members may be indicated.

GENERALIZED ANXIETY DISORDER

Thomas is a 25-year-old married mechanic who experiences persistent worry about a variety of situations. Sometimes at work he worries that he has left the gas stove turned on in his house. He worries about his wife commuting to work and about the babysitter's ability to care for their child. He often has shaky hands, a dry mouth, and trouble sleeping. When he developed severe heartburn, his physician prescribed a low dosage of benzodiazepines.

Tom has a generalized anxiety disorder (GAD), a generalized and persistent anxiety without any of the characteristics of other anxiety disorders. That is, he does not have sudden anxiety in the presence of a feared object, and there are no obsessions or compulsions, no panic attacks, and no numbing/denial pattern as found in PTSD.

The *DSM-IV* defines GAD in part as "excessive anxiety and worry (apprehensive expectation), occurring more days than not for a period of at least 6 months, about a number of events or activities" (American Psychiatric Association, 1994, p. 432). The symptoms of GAD include (a) motor tension such as trembling and restlessness; (b) autonomic hyperactivity characterized by symptoms such as shortness of breath, sweating, dry mouth, nausea, and so on; and (c) vigilance and scanning.

Generalized anxiety disorder has undergone substantial clarification since it was first introduced in *DSM-III*. Then it was considered a residual category consisting of generalized and persistent anxiety without any of the characteristics of the other anxiety disorders. However, the old definition of GAD had low inter-rater reliabilities (kappa coefficients around .47 to .57), primarily because clinicians differed in their interpretations of the degree of anxiety present and/or the length of time that the patient had the anxiety.

Subsequent research has improved the specificity of the disorder and should lead to greater inter-rater reliability. Research now suggests that GAD is not just a residual category, but is best described as a disorder characterized by apprehensive expectation. Thus it can be best described as a disorder with certain cardinal features as opposed to a disorder defined by what it does not have. The *DSM-IV* (American Psychiatric Association, 1994) reflects this improved thinking and suggests that the symptoms of GAD include pervasive worry that is focused on many life-circumstances and with an intensity that "is far out of proportion to the actual likelihood or impact of the feared event" (American Psychiatric Association, 1994, p. 433).

Barlow (1988) noted that many anxiety patients appear to meet the diagnosis of GAD, except that they have only one focus of worry. A useful heuristic might be to treat these patients in the same manner as patients who meet the full criteria for GAD.

Generalized anxiety disorder may start at any age. Studies listing the mean age of onset vary widely from the mid-teens to the 30s (Rapee, 1991). The sex distribution is about equal (Thyer, Parrish, et al., 1985). Although it is psychologically taxing, uncomplicated GAD generally does not show the degree of impairment common to other anxiety disorders. However, GAD in combination with other anxiety disorders or major depression can be quite debilitating. Massion, Warshaw, and Keller (1993) found that 37% of the patients with GAD (most of whom had other coexisting disorders) were on disability, unemployment, or social security.

DIFFERENTIAL DIAGNOSIS

Relatively few patients receive a primary diagnosis of GAD. At the Center for Stress and Anxiety disorders at Albany, New York, only about 11% of the patients received a primary diagnosis of GAD (Barlow et al., 1986). This rate corresponds roughly to that found at other anxiety disorder centers.

In some respects, almost all anxiety disorder patients could receive GAD as a diagnosis because most anxious patients experience some of the GAD symptoms. The only exception is specific phobias, where only 40% of those patients meet the criterion for GAD. Massion et al. (1993) found that 78% of the patients with GAD had a concurrent diagnosis of another anxiety disorder or major depression.

However, with the emphasis on pervasive vigilance it should be easier to distinguish the anxiety found in GAD from the anticipatory anxiety found in other anxiety disorders, especially panic disorders. Panic disorder patients frequently fear the next panic attack (anticipatory anxiety), while GAD patients express anxiety about multiple life circumstances.

GAD differs from panic disorders in other ways as well. Although GAD patients sometimes have panic attacks, the attacks are not frequent and do not lead to territorial apprehensiveness. Also, GAD patients experience fewer autonomic symptoms, and the onset of the disorder is earlier and more gradual than the onset of panic disorder. Furthermore, relatives of panic disorder patients have a higher than average incidence of GAD among their family members. To date, convincing evidence for a biological etiology of GAD is lacking (Marks, 1987). Finally, although GAD tends to be chronic and unfluctuating, it appears to be more benign and easier to treat than panic disorders.

The number of GAD patients with coexisting personality disorders has been measured at 18% (Klass et al., 1989) to 41% (Mauri et al., 1992). The majority of the personality disorders fall into the anxious/dependent cluster (Mauri et al., 1992).

TREATMENTS FOR GAD

Because GAD is a relatively new disorder, first classified in *DSM-III*, there are few outcome studies with it. Many pre-*DSM-III* studies probably included panic-disordered subjects. Nevertheless, this research suggests that GAD may respond to a number of interventions, including biofeedback, relaxation training, cognitive restructuring, and combined packages.

It is difficult to pick one of these interventions over another because each of them involves teaching relaxation as a self-control skill to apply in a wide range of situations. Systematic desensitization, which is primarily applied to classically conditioned fears, does not appear useful to GAD, except if the patient has a coexisting specific or social phobia.

Cognitive procedures such as outlined by Beck and Emery (1985), Ellis (Whalen et al., 1980), or Meichenbaum (1977) may be helpful for GAD problems by modifying the dysfunctional thoughts that characterize the disorder. In their review of outcome studies, Chambless and Gillis (1993) found that cognitive-behavioral treatments were consistently superior to waiting list and placebo groups. Nonetheless, some authors (e.g., Rapee,

67

1991) have concluded that relaxation, biofeedback, and cognitive restructuring produce limited improvements when used alone.

Benzodiazepines seem to reduce autonomic disturbance and have few drug interactions and side-effects except for occasional drowsiness. A major question, however, concerns the abuse of benzodiazepines and possible addiction. Whereas some believe that benzodiazepines are widely abused and that long-term use is not indicated, others believe that they are safe at commonly pre-scribed low levels and that long-term use does not necessarily lead to dependency or addiction. Perhaps the greatest abuse of benzodiazepines is to prescribe them without also offering psy-chotherapy directed at altering stressful life situations. Would the use of benzodiazepines to reduce anxiety encourage someone to stay at an unpleasant job or in an abusive relationship? If so, then medication alone is contraindicated.

Persons with a past history of drug and alcohol abuse are highly vulnerable to abuse benzodiazepines, in which case a low dose of neuroleptics or antidepressants with incidental anxiety-reducing features may be indicated.

Despite disputes concerning the long-term use of benzodiaze-pines, there is little controversy that short-term low dose use can help GAD patients. Recent studies suggest that tricyclic antide-pressants or buspirone may be helpful for GAD without some of the shortcomings of benzodiazepines.

A CASE VIGNETTE

Donna is a 46-year-old lawyer with a prestigious law firm. She has a reputation for being meticulous and for researching her cases thoroughly. Some of her clients re-quested another lawyer because she took so long to pre-pare their cases. Occasionally her extreme carefulness paid off, and she found an unusual legal precedent or theory which made a difference in court. She would usu-ally develop somatic anxiety while worrying about the de-tails of case preparation. Donna was not satisfied with her performance and continually worried about doing the best job she could. She had trouble sleeping at night, and often returned to work after hours to check and double check the references and style of writing in her briefs. Her worries were not confined to work. She often ruminated unnecessarily about her children's health or family finances.

Diagnosis and Treatment Recommendations

Diagnosis.   Axis I: Generalized Anxiety Disorder
              Axis II: Insufficient Information

Treatment Plan.   Donna demonstrates hypervigilance and anxiety that has generalized to a wide range of situations. She shows some signs of compulsivity in that her perfectionism at work interferes with job performance. At this point it is not clear whether the perfectionism is an enduring trait or a consequence of anxiety about job performance. Although Donna did report some vegetative symptoms of anxiety, she emphasized vigilance and apprehensive expectation. On the basis of this information, a cognitive approach appears indicated.

CHILDREN'S ANXIETY DISORDERS

Sally is a third grader who refuses to go to school. At first she complained that she was sick. Although the pediatrician accepted her vague symptoms as legitimate at first, it eventually became clear that there was nothing physically wrong with her. At times her mother has tried to make her go to school, but Sally cries, fights, and rebels until her mother lets her stay home. Sally's refusal is a mystery to her teacher, who has found her to be well-behaved, polite, and above-average in school performance.

The *DSM-III-R* lists several different anxiety disorders unique to children: separation anxiety disorder, overanxious disorder, and avoidant disorders of childhood or adolescence. We provide special attention to separation anxiety disorder because overanxious disorder and avoidant disorders of childhood have near equivalents in the adult GAD and avoidant personality disorder described previously.

Of course children may experience any of the other anxiety disorders as well. Even panic disorder has been diagnosed in children, although this is rare (see Kearney & Silverman, 1992, for a critical review of panic disorder in adolescents). Children usually have specific phobias, obsessive-compulsive disorders, and post-traumatic stress disorder. As with adults, children with anxiety disorders are at greater risk to develop depression and to abuse alcohol and other drugs. Although the diagnostic criteria are the same for children as for adults, these disorders have unique features in children that have treatment implications.

SEPARATION ANXIETY DISORDER

The *DSM-III-R* defines separation anxiety disorder as "excessive anxiety, for at least two weeks, concerning separation from those to whom the child is attached" (American Psychiatric Association, 1987, p. 58). It is characterized by at least three of the following: (a) unrealistic fear of harm to parents, guardians, or loved ones; (b) unrealistic worry about calamitous events; (c) persistent reluctance or refusal to go to school or leave home; (d) refusal to go to sleep without parents nearby; (e) vague physical complaints on school days; (f) excessive distress upon separation from parents; (g) repeated nightmares concerning separation; (h) recurrent complaints of excessive distress in anticipation of separation from home and parents; or (i) fear of being away from home alone.

It is common for children to show fear of unfamiliar circumstances such as a new day care center or a new teacher. Often children will balk temporarily at having to go to school. Firm insistence and emotional support from parents is sufficient to eliminate this fear in the vast majority of children. Separation anxiety disorders should only be diagnosed when the school refusal is persistent and the other *DSM-III-R* criteria are met.

Often the separation anxiety disorder is precipitated by an illness suffered by the child, death or illness of a person in the child's home, divorce of the parents, or a change of schedule. The disorder is more common after a change of school buildings, a family move, promotion from elementary to middle school, or long vacations or illnesses. Unfortunately, the parents may inadvertently reinforce the separation anxiety by catering to the "sick" child or exaggerating the difficulties at school.

Children with separation anxiety disorder are more likely to be female, prepubertal, and from lower socioeconomic backgrounds. Their mothers are more likely to suffer from major depressions or anxiety disorders than mothers of other children, and one-third of separation anxiety children also can be diagnosed as having overanxious disorder (Last et al., 1987). It is believed to be the most common of all childhood anxiety disorders.

Differential Diagnosis. The correct diagnosis of separation anxiety disorder requires the differentiation of the reasons for failure to attend school or leave the parents. In the past, many clinicians failed to distinguish separation anxiety from a fear (phobia) of something in school. If the child has an actual fear of something in school, then specific phobia may be the proper diagnosis. In other cases the child may have avoidant disorder of childhood (which implies a fear of strangers), may experience social anxiety, or may be subjected to an unfriendly or harsh environment in school.

Separation anxiety disorder also requires a differentiation from other disorders such as major depression and conduct disorder. In major depression, the symptoms of separation anxiety disorder exist along with symptoms of depression such as loss of appetite, insomnia, fatigue, and melancholia and continue even when the parents are present. Psychotherapists also need to distinguish separation anxiety disorder from conduct disorders. Some school refusals are part of a pattern in which the rights of others are chronically violated. Although conduct disorder children may refuse to go to school, they are not excessively attached to their parents and typically are not cooperative in other aspects of family life.

The patient having separation anxiety disorder has a good prognosis unless the condition is chronic. The optimal interventions, whether they include family therapy, behavior therapy, or others, all involve getting the child back to the school environment as soon as possible. Although the child may resist at first, failing to place the child back in school only makes treatment more difficult later, and adjustment to school is usually adequate. Because parents are likely to have difficulty insisting on school attendance, they usually need emotional support. As noted previously, many of the mothers also have depression or anxiety and may require concurrent treatment.

Imipramine has had some success with separation anxiety disorder, but evidence of its superiority over behavior therapy is lacking.

Some authors have opined that children with separation anxiety disorder are at an increased risk to develop agoraphobia or panic disorder. However, no longitudinal studies have been conducted to test this hypothesis.

OVERANXIOUS DISORDER

The overanxious disorder of childhood is characterized by at least four of the following: (a) unrealistic worry about the future; (b) preoccupation with the appropriateness of past behavior; (c) overconcern with competence in school or other tasks; (d) excessive need for reassurance; (e) physical complaints; (f) marked self-consciousness or tendency to be easily embarrassed; or (g) severe feelings of tension or inability to relax. This disorder appeared first in the *DSM-III*, and few studies or data are available. It appears to correspond roughly to that of GAD in adults. The classification from which it is most likely to require differentiation is adjustment disorder with anxious mood, in which the child has transitory symptoms precipitated by a stressful life change.

Until we learn more, treatment should follow the same pattern as GAD with adults, emphasizing cognitive reassurance and relaxation techniques modified for children (Koeppen, 1974). Parental involvement is usually needed to insure practice of relaxation exercises, to reinforce cognitive changes, and to alter parental patterns which may inadvertently exacerbate the disorder. Cognitive strategies for children may involve bibliotherapy (Sarafino, 1986) or mutual story-tellings, and parents may need to learn listening techniques so they can better understand their child's concerns.

AVOIDANT DISORDERS OF
CHILDHOOD OR ADOLESCENCE

The *DSM-III-R* defines the avoidant disorder as "an excessive shrinking from contact with unfamiliar people that is of sufficient severity to interfere with social functioning in peer relationships and that is of at least six months' duration" (American Psychiatric Association, 1987, p. 61). In addition, these children show a clear desire for social interactions with familiar people, and relationships with family members are warm and satisfying.

This disorder was also new to the *DSM-III*, and no studies or data are available. It appears to correspond roughly to avoidant personality disorder in adults and is most likely to require differentiation from separation anxiety disorder. In separation anxiety disorder the child has no fear of strangers when accompanied by parents or guardians, whereas in avoidance disorder, the child is afraid of strangers in most situations. Also, the anxiety is not pervasive, as in overanxious disorders, and is limited to contact with strangers. Because it appears to be a mild or early version of avoidant personality disorder, the psychotherapist should look for traits that characterize avoidant personality disorder, such as low self-esteem and poor social skills.

No treatment outcome studies are available yet. Nevertheless, the nature of the disorder suggests that some of the procedures used for the treatment of social phobia may be indicated: relaxation, cognitive restructuring, and social skills training. As always with children, extensive parental involvement is required, and strategies need to be modified for the child's developmental level.

CHILDHOOD EQUIVALENTS
OF ADULT DISORDERS

Children can have specific phobias, obsessive-compulsive disorders, or post-traumatic stress disorders, but panic disorders are very rare (Nelles & Barlow, 1988) and we will not discuss them. The nature of childhood phobias varies according to the developmental stage of the child. As a rule, young children tend to fear physical harm from such sources as dogs or large animals, whereas older children fear social embarrassment in situations such as a bully's intimidation or rejection by schoolmates or teachers. In part, this differing pattern of fears occurs because the older child has different social demands like attending school and being exposed to a wider range of people than the younger child. Girls tend to report more fears than boys, although this may be due to sex role stereotypes which allow girls more latitude in expressing fear.

Transient childhood fears are very common, and psychotherapists need to differentiate specific phobias from normal fears. Normal fears tend to be more age specific, to create relatively less fear, to be amenable to normal reassurance, and to subside within 2 years without treatment.

The treatment of childhood phobias corresponds roughly to the treatment for specific phobias for adults (Johnson, 1985). As with other childhood disorders, the psychotherapist must emphasize family and environmental variables that may inadvertently maintain or create the phobia. A parent who shows extreme anxiety may be modeling fear for the child, or a sibling who teases or misinforms a younger child may have induced a phobia. Parents may also contribute to creating a phobia by "protecting" the child from normal situations that would engender moderate anxiety in any child.

Systematic desensitization modified for children has been effective, but the therapist can also rely on a variety of modeling and operant conditioning procedures. Because the parents have so much control over their child's environment, well-constructed programs like this usually succeed. Of course, skill acquisition techniques, such as animal management for overcoming fear of dogs, may help some children conquer their phobias.

Obsessive-compulsive disorders often start in childhood, especially in early adolescence. The treatment procedures are the same with children as with adults, and education of the parents is crucial. Parents need to understand the nature of the treatments and, if the treatment is response prevention, how these procedures may temporarily create some anxiety. Their failure to participate in the program as instructed will subvert the therapeutic effort and lead to future demoralization. Clinicians should be aware of the high co-morbidity of OCD with Tourette's and other tic disorders.

Post-traumatic stress disorder can occur at any age. The *DSM-III-R* and *DSM-IV* recognize unique PTSD symptoms that can occur in children such as repetitive play, drawings, or dreams of the traumatic event. Diminished interest in activities and constriction of emotions are difficult for young children to report, and careful evaluation of symptoms by parents, teachers, and others is warranted.

A child's reactions to trauma used to be attributed partly to parental reactions, although massive trauma can cause PTSD in children independent of parental reactions (Eth & Pynoos, 1985) and its effects may depend on the age, sex, developmental level of the child, or the nature of the trauma. Nevertheless, the research is not conclusive about the differential effects on children (Eth & Pynoos, 1985).

A CASE VIGNETTE

> Shelly is a 4-year-old who is afraid to go to sleep at night. She will not even go upstairs to her room alone. The fear began a year ago after she saw a bat in her room. Shortly thereafter, her older brother began to tease her about ghosts and monsters at night. Her parents have been unable to persuade her to go to sleep by herself, and she insists on sleeping in their bedroom. Shelly becomes very upset if she is pressured to sleep alone. If they move her to her room in the middle of the night, while asleep, she will go back to her parents' room immediately when she wakens.

Diagnosis and Treatment Recommendations

Diagnosis.   Axis I: Specific Phobia

Treatment Plan. Although childhood fears are common, this fear is interfering with Shelly's daily functioning, thus warranting the diagnosis of specific phobia. Because the phobia appears to have been created by a cognitive misinterpretation of the danger of bats and monsters, we recommend a multimodal treatment that would involve cognitive restructuring, positive reinforcement, and graduated exposure. The cognitive restructuring is modified to a child's perspective and could involve reading children's books about monsters and fears (see Sarafino [1986] for recommendations of several appropriate books). The parents can play games

75

with Shelly in which ghosts, monsters, and other imaginary creatures are mocked and treated as make-believe. Of course the older brother needs to stop telling ghost stories. Through graduated exposure, Shelly can spend more and more time upstairs alone with positive reinforcements given for "brave" behaviors.

SUMMARY

The *DSM-III-R* reflected substantial improvement in the diagnosis of anxiety disorders. A recurrent theme of this guide, however, is that the basic *DSM-III-R* and *DSM-IV* labels are not sufficient to select the optimal treatment. Instead, the psychotherapist may need to know the origins of the anxiety disorder, the coexistence of other disorders, or other characteristics and assets of the patients. The authors have presented research to make the treatment decisions as explicit as possible. Psychotherapists must add their clinical judgment to this empirical data in making the treatment decisions.

APPENDICES

APPENDIX A: AGORAPHOBIC
COGNITIONS QUESTIONNAIRE*

Below are some thoughts or ideas that may pass through your mind when you are nervous or frightened.

Indicate how often each thought occurs when you are nervous. Rate from 1 to 5 using the scale below.

1 = Thought never occurs.

2 = Thought rarely occurs.

3 = Thought occurs during half of the time I am nervous.

4 = Thought usually occurs.

5 = Thought always occurs when I am nervous.

_1_ 1. I am going to throw up.

_2_ 2. I am going to pass out.

_5_ 3. I must have a brain tumor.

_5_ 4. I will have a heart attack.

_3_ 5. I will choke to death.

_5_ 6. I am going to act foolish.

_3_ 7. I am going blind.

_5_ 8. I will not be able to control myself.

_5_ 9. I will hurt someone.

_5_ 10. I am going to have a stroke.

---

*Note: From "Assessment of Fear in Agoraphobia: The Body Sensations Questionnaire and the Agoraphobic Cognitions Questionnaire" by D. Chambless, G. Caputo, P. Bright, and R. Gallagher, 1984, *Journal of Consulting and Clinical Psychology, 52,* pp. 1090-1097. Copyright © 1984 by the Pergamon Journals, Ltd. Reprinted by permission.

_6_ 11. I am going to go crazy.

_5_ 12. I am going to scream.

_6_ 13. I am going to babble or talk funny.

_3_ 14. I will be paralyzed by fear.

_1_ 15. OTHER IDEAS NOT LISTED (Please describe and rate them)

The total score is derived by averaging all the responses. Panic disorder patients average 2.8 (*SD* = .8) before treatment and 2.1 (*SD* = .9) 6 months after treatment.

APPENDIX B: BODY
SENSATIONS QUESTIONNAIRE*

Below is a list of specific body sensations that may occur when you are nervous or in a feared situation. Please mark down how afraid you are of these feelings. Use a five-point scale from Not frightened to Extremely frightened.

1 = Not frightened or worried by this sensation.

2 = Somewhat frightened by this sensation.

3 = Moderately frightened by this sensation.

4 = Very frightened by this sensation.

5 = Extremely frightened by this sensation.

1	1.	Heart palpitations
4	2.	Pressure or a heavy feeling in chest
5	3.	Numbness in arms or legs
5	4.	Tingling in the fingertips
5	5.	Numbness in another part of your body
5	6.	Feeling short of breath
5	7.	Dizziness
2	8.	Blurred or distorted vision
5	9.	Nausea
5	10.	Having "butterflies" in your stomach
3	11.	Feeling a knot in your stomach
1	12.	Having a lump in your throat
4	13.	Wobbly or rubber legs
1	14.	Sweating

*Note: From "Assessment of Fear in Agoraphobia: The Body Sensations Questionnaire and the Agoraphobic Cognitions Questionnaire" by D. Chambless, G. Caputo, P. Bright, and R. Gallagher, 1984, *Journal of Consulting and Clinical Psychology, 52,* pp. 1090-1097. Copyright © 1984 by the Pergamon Journals, Ltd. Reprinted by permission.

_4_ 15. A dry throat

_5_ 16. Feeling disoriented and confused

_2_ 17. Feeling disconnected from your body: only partly present

_____ 18. Other _____

               Please describe _____

_____

The total score is derived by averaging responses across individual items. Panic disorder patients average 2.9 (*SD* = 1.3) before treatment and 1.7 (*SD* = 1.0) 6 months after treatment.

APPENDIX C: MOBILITY
INVENTORY FOR AGORAPHOBIA*

Name: _____   Date: _____

1. Please indicate the degree to which you avoid the following places
    or situations because of discomfort or anxiety. Rate your amount of
    avoidance when you are with a trusted companion and when you are
    alone. Do this by using the following scale.

                1 = Never avoid
                2 = Rarely avoid
                3 = Avoid about half the time
                4 = Avoid most of the time
                5 = Always avoid

    (You may use numbers halfway between those listed when
    you think it is appropriate. For example, 3.5 or 4.5.)

    Write your score in the blanks for each situation or place under both
    conditions: When Accompanied and When Alone. Leave blank
    situations that do not apply to you.

2. After completing the first step, circle the five items with which you
    are most concerned. Of the items listed, these are the five situations
    or places where avoidance/anxiety most affects your life in a nega-
    tive way.

Places	When Accompanied	When Alone
Theatres	1	4
Supermarkets	1	2
Classrooms	1	2

*Note: From "The Mobility Inventory for Agoraphobia" by D. Chambless, G. Caputo, S. Ja-
sin, E. Gracely, and C. Williams, 1985, *Behaviour Research and Therapy, 23,* pp. 35-44.
Copyright © by the Pergamon Journals, Ltd. Reprinted by permission.

Anxiety Disorders

Places	When Accompanied	When Alone
Department Stores	1	3
Restaurants	1	4
Museums	1	1
Elevators	1	1
Auditoriums or Stadiums	1	1
Garages	1	1
High Places Please tell how high _____	1	1

Enclosed Spaces

	When Accompanied	When Alone
For Example, Tunnels	1	3

Open Spaces

	When Accompanied	When Alone
Outside (e.g., fields, wide streets, courtyards)	1	1
Inside (e.g., large rooms, lobbies)	1	1

Riding In

	When Accompanied	When Alone
Buses	1	1
Trains	1	1
Subways	1	1
Boats	1	1

Driving or Riding in Car
    At Any Time
    On Expressways
	2
	2
		5
		5

Anxiety Disorders

Places	When Accompanied	When Alone
Situations		
Standing in Lines	N/A	N/A
Crossing Bridges	N/A	2
Parties or Social Gatherings	N/A	5
Walking on the Street	N/A	3
Staying at Home Alone	N/A	2
Being Far Away from Home	N/A	4
Other (specify)		
_____	_____	_____

Panic disorder patients average 2.3 ($SD = .9$) on the Avoidance When Accompanied subscale before treatment and 1.5 ($SD = .6$) 6 months after treatment. They average 3.4 ($SD = 1.0$) on the Avoidance Alone subscale before treatment and 2.2 ($SD = 1.4$) 6 months after treatment.

We define a *panic attack* as:

1. A high level of anxiety accompanied by
2. strong body reactions (heart palpitations, sweating, muscle tremors, dizziness, nausea) with
3. the temporary loss of the ability to plan, think, or reason and
4. the intense desire to escape or flee the situation. (Note: This is different from high anxiety or fear alone.)

Please indicate the total number of panic attacks you have had in the last 7 days. ____2____

On the average, how severe or intense have the panic attacks been?

1. Very mild _____
2. Mild X_____
3. Moderately severe _____
4. Very severe _____
5. Extremely severe _____

85

The data on a sample of 232 outpatients with a diagnosis of agoraphobia with panic attacks produced a normal distribution of scores with a mean of 3.19 ($SD = 1.00$).

SAFETY ZONE

Many people are able to travel alone freely in an area (usually around their home) called their safety zone. Do you have such a zone? _____

If yes, describe:

1. its location: At *school and at home, on my way home using only my daily route.*

2. its size (e.g., radius from home): *miles*

APPENDIX D: FEAR QUESTIONNAIRE*

Choose a number from the scale below to show how much you would avoid each of the situations listed below because of fear or other unpleasant feelings. Then circle the number you chose opposite each situation.

0	1	2	3	4	5	6	7	8
Would not avoid it		Slightly avoid it		Definitely avoid it		Markedly avoid it		Always avoid it

1. Main phobia you want treated
   (describe in your own words):_____

2. Injections or minor surgery........ 0 1 ② 3 4 5 6 7 8

3. Eating or drinking with
   other people.............................. 0 ① 2 3 4 5 6 7 8

4. Hospitals.................................... 0 1 2 3 ④ 5 6 7 8

5. Traveling alone by bus
   or coach................................... 0 1 ② 3 4 5 6 7 8

6. Walking alone in busy street...... ⓪ 1 2 3 4 5 6 7 8

7. Being watched or stared at......... 0 ① 2 3 4 5 6 7 8

8. Going into crowded shops.......... ⓪ 1 2 3 4 5 6 7 8

9. Talking to people in authority.... 0 1 2 3 4 5 6 7 8

10. Sight of blood........................... ⓪ 1 2 3 4 5 6 7 8

11. Being criticized......................... 0 1 2 3 4 5 6 7 ⑧

12. Going alone far from home........ 0 1 2 3 4 5 6 ⑦ 8

13. Thought of injury or illness....... ⓪ 1 2 3 4 5 6 7 8

*Note: From "Brief Standard Self-Rating for Phobic Patients" by I. M. Marks and A. M. Matthews, 1979, *Behaviour Research and Therapy, 17,* pp. 263-267. Copyright © 1979 by the Pergamon Journals, Ltd. Reprinted by permission.

14. Speaking or acting
    before an audience...................... 0 1 2 3 4 5 6 7 8

15. Large open spaces...................... 0 1 2 3 4 5 6 7 8

16. Going to the dentist...................... 0 1 2 3 4 5 6 7 8

17. Other situations (describe).......... 0 1 2 3 4 5 6 7 8

                                        TOTAL _____

Now choose a number from the scale below to show how much you are troubled by each problem listed, and circle the number.

0	1	2	3	4	5	6	7	8
Hardly at all		Slightly troublesome		Definitely troublesome		Markedly troublesome		Very severely troublesome

18. Feeling miserable or depressed.. 0 1 2 3 4 5 6 7 8

19. Feeling irritable or angry............ 0 1 2 3 4 5 6 7 8

20. Feeling tense or panicky............. 0 1 2 3 4 5 6 7 8

21. Upsetting thoughts coming into
    your mind................................. 0 1 2 3 4 5 6 7 8

22. Feeling you or your surround-
    ings are strange or unreal........... 0 1 2 3 4 5 6 7 8

23. Other feelings (describe)........... 0 1 2 3 4 5 6 7 8

                                        TOTAL _____

How would you rate the present state of your phobic symptoms on the scale below?

0	1	2	3	4	5	6	7	8
No phobias present		Slightly disturbing/ not really disabling		Definitely disturbing/ disabling		Markedly disturbing/ disabling		Very severely disturbing/ disabling

Please circle one number between 0 and 8.

APPENDIX E: MAUDSLEY OBSESSIONAL-COMPULSIVE (MOC) INVENTORY*

1 = Checking; 2 = Cleaning; 3 = Slowness; 4 = Doubting

Note: Subscales have unequal number of items.

	Subscale
1. I avoid using public telephones because of possible contamination.	2
2. I frequently get nasty thoughts and have difficulty getting rid of them.	3
3. I am more concerned than most people about honesty.	4
4. I am often late because I can't seem to get through everything on time.	2
5. I don't worry unduly about contamination if I touch an animal.	2
6. I frequently have to check things (e.g., gas or water taps, doors, etc.) several times.	1
7. I have a very strict conscience.	4
8. I find that almost every day I am upset by unpleasant thoughts that come into my mind against my will.	1
9. I do not worry unduly if I accidentally bump into somebody.	2
10. I usually have serious doubts about the simple everyday things I do.	4
11. Neither of my parents were very strict during my childhood.	4
12. I tend to get behind in my work because I repeat things over and over again.	4

*Note: From "Obsessional Compulsive Complaints" by R. J. Hodgson and S. Rachman, 1977, *Behaviour Research and Therapy, 15,* pp. 389-395. Copyright © 1977 by the Pergamon Journals, Ltd. Reprinted by permission.

	Subscale
13. I use only an average amount of soap.	2
14. Some numbers are extremely unlucky.	1
15. I do not check letters over and over again before posting them.	1
16. I do not take a long time to dress in the morning.	3
17. I am not excessively concerned about cleanliness.	2
18. One of my major problems is that I pay too much attention to detail.	4
19. I can use well-kept toilets without any hesitation.	2
20. My major problem is repeated checking.	1
21. I am not unduly concerned about germs and diseases.	2
22. I do not tend to check things more than once.	1
23. I do not stick to a very strict routine when doing ordinary things.	3
24. My hands do not feel dirty after touching money.	2
25. I do not usually count when doing a routine task.	3
26. I take rather a long time to complete my washing in the morning.	2
27. I do not use a great deal of antiseptics.	2
28. I spend a lot of time every day checking things over and over again.	1
29. Hanging and folding my clothes at night does not take up a lot of time.	3
30. Even when I do something very carefully I often feel that it is not quite right.	3

REFERENCES

American Psychiatric Association. (1980). *Diagnostic and Statistical Manual of Mental Disorders* (3rd ed.). Washington, DC: Author.

American Psychiatric Association. (1987). *Diagnostic and Statistical Manual of Mental Disorders* (3rd ed. rev.). Washington, DC: Author.

American Psychiatric Association. (1994). *Diagnostic and Statistical Manual of Mental Disorders* (4th ed.). Washington, DC: Author.

Bard, M., & Sangry, D. (1986). *The Crime Victim's Book* (2nd ed.). New York: Brunner/Mazel.

Barlow, D. (1988). *Anxiety and Its Disorders: The Nature and Treatment of Anxiety.* New York: Guilford.

Barlow, D., DiNardo, P., Vermilyea, B., Vermilyea, J., & Blanchard, E. (1986). Co-morbidity and depression among the anxiety disorders: Issues in diagnosis and classification. *The Journal of Nervous and Mental Disease, 174,* 63-72.

Barlow, D., & Waddell, M. (1985). Agoraphobia. In D. Barlow (Ed.), *Clinical Handbook of Psychological Disorders* (pp. 1-68). New York: Guilford.

Barlow, D., & Wolfe, B. (1981). Behavioral approaches to anxiety disorders: A report on the NIMH-SUNY, Albany Research Conference. *Journal of Consulting and Clinical Psychology, 40,* 448-454.

Barrios, B., & Shigetomi, C. (1979). Coping skills training for the management of anxiety: A critical review. *Behavior Therapy, 10,* 491-522.

Beck, A. T., & Emery, G. (1985). *Anxiety Disorders and Phobias: A Cognitive Perspective.* New York: Basic Books.

Beck, A. T., Ward, C. H., Mendelson, M., Mock, J., & Erbaugh, J. (1961). An inventory for measuring depression. *Archives of General Psychiatry, 4,* 561-571.

Bernstein, D., & Borkovec, T. (1974). *Progressive Muscle Relaxation: A Manual for the Helping Professions.* Champaign, IL: Research Press.

Bernstein, G., & Borchardt, C. (1991). Anxiety disorders of childhood and adolescence: A critical review. *Journal of the Academy of Child and Adolescent Psychiatry, 30,* 519-532.

Black, D., Yates, W., Noyes, R., Pfohl, B., & Kelly, M. (1989). DSM-III Personality disorder in obsessive-compulsive study volunteers: A controlled study. *Journal of Personality Disorders, 3,* 58-62.

Blanchard, E., Gerardi, R., Kolb, L., & Barlow, D. (1986). The utility of the Anxiety Disorders Interview Schedule (ADIS) in the diagnosis of Post-Traumatic Stress Disorder (PTSD) in Vietnam veterans. *Behaviour Research and Therapy, 24,* 577-580.

Boulenger, J.-P., & Lavallee, Y.-J. (1993). Mixed anxiety and depression: Diagnostic issues. *Journal of Clinical Psychiatry, 54*(Suppl. 1), 3-8.

Brown, T., & Barlow, D. (1992). Comorbidity among anxiety disorders: Implications for treatment and DSM-IV. *Journal of Consulting and Clinical Psychology, 60,* 835-844.

Cameron, O., Thyer, B., Neese, R., & Curtis, G. (1986). Symptom profiles of patients with DSM-III anxiety disorders. *American Journal of Psychiatry, 143,* 1132-1137.

Cerny, J., Himadi, W., & Barlow, D. (1984). Issues in diagnosing anxiety disorders. *Journal of Behavioral Assessment, 6,* 301-329.

Chambless, D., Caputo, G., Bright, P., & Gallagher, R. (1984). Assessment of fear in agoraphobia: The Body Sensations Questionnaire and the Agoraphobic Cognitions Questionnaire. *Journal of Consulting and Clinical Psychology, 52,* 1090-1097.

Chambless, D., Caputo, G., Jasin, S., Gracely, E., & Williams, C. (1985). The Mobility Inventory for Agoraphobia. *Behaviour Research and Therapy, 23,* 35-44.

Chambless, D., & Gillis, M. (1993). Cognitive therapy of anxiety disorders. *Journal of Consulting and Clinical Psychology, 61,* 248-260.

Chapman, T., Fyer, A., Mannuzza, S., & Klein, D. (1993). A comparison of treated and untreated simple phobia. *American Journal of Psychiatry, 150,* 816-818.

Clarke, J. C., & Wardman, W. (1985). *Agoraphobia: A Clinical and Personal Account.* Sydney, Australia: Pergamon.

Clarkin, J., & Kendall, P. (1992). Comorbidity and treatment planning: Summary and future directions. *Journal of Consulting and Clinical Psychology, 60,* 904-908.

Cooper, T. (1970). The Leyton Obsessional Inventory. *Psychological Medicine, 1,* 48-64.

Cox, B., Endler, N., Lee, P., & Swinson, R. (1992). A meta-analysis of treatments for panic disorder with agoraphobia: Imipramine, alprazolam, and in vivo exposure. *Journal of Behavior Therapy and Experimental Psychiatry, 23,* 175-182.

DiNardo, P., O'Brien, G., Barlow, D., Waddell, M., & Blanchard, E. (1983). Reliability of DSM-III anxiety disorder categories using a new structured interview. *Archives of General Psychiatry, 40,* 1070-1074.

Dubovsky, S. (1990). Generalized anxiety disorder: New concepts and psychopharmacologic therapies. *Journal of Clinical Psychiatry, 51*(Suppl.), 3-10.

Eth, S., & Pynoos, R. (1985). *Post-Traumatic Stress Disorder in Children.* Washington, DC: American Psychiatric Association Press.

Fairbanks, J., Keane, T., & Malloy, P. (1983). Some preliminary data on the psychological characteristics of Vietnam veterans with post-traumatic stress disorder. *Journal of Consulting and Clinical Psychology, 51,* 912-919.

Fairbanks, J., & Nicholson, R. (1987). Theoretical and empirical issues in the treatment of post-traumatic stress disorder in Vietnam veterans. *Journal of Clinical Psychology, 43,* 44-55.

Fight to conquer fear. (1984, April 23). *Newsweek, 103,* 66-72.

Friedman, C., Shear, M. L., & Frances, A. (1987). DSM-III personality disorders in panic patients. *Journal of Personality Disorders, 1,* 132-135.

Gibbs, M. (1989). Factors in the victim that mediate between disaster and psychopathology: A review. *Journal of Traumatic Stress, 3,* 489-514.

Goldfried, M., & Trier, C. (1974). Effectiveness of relaxation as an active coping skill. *Journal of Abnormal Psychology, 83,* 348-355.

Goldstein, S. (1986). Sequential treatment of panic disorder with alprazolam and imipramine. *American Journal of Psychiatry, 143,* 1634.

Goodman, W., McDougle, C., & Price, L. (1992). Pharmacotherapy of obsessive compulsive behavior. *Journal of Clinical Psychiatry, 53*(Suppl. 4), 29-37.

Gorton, G., & Akhtar, S. (1990). The literature on personality disorders, 1985-1988: Trends, issues, and controversies. *Hospital and Community Psychiatry, 41,* 39-51.

Green, B., Lindy, J., & Grace, M. (1985). Posttraumatic stress disorder: Toward DSM-IV. *The Journal of Nervous and Mental Disease, 173,* 406-411.

Green, M., & Curtis, G. (1988). Personality disorders in panic patients: Response to termination of antipanic medication. *Journal of Personality Disorders, 2,* 303-314.

Greist, J. (1992). An integrated approach to treatment of obsessive compulsive disorder. *Journal of Clinical Psychiatry, 53*(Suppl. 4), 38-41.

Grieger, R., & Boyd, J. (1980). *Rational-Emotive Therapy: A Skill Based Approach.* New York: Van Nostrand.

Heimberg, R. (1989). Cognitive and behavioral treatments for social phobia: A critical analysis. *Clinical Psychology Review, 9,* 107-128.

Heimberg, R., & Barlow, D. (1988). Psychosocial treatments for social phobia. *Psychosomatics, 29,* 27-37.

Heimberg, R., Hope, D., Dodge, C., & Becker, R. (1990). DSM-III-R subtypes of social phobia: Comparison of generalized social phobics and public speaking phobics. *The Journal of Nervous and Mental Disease, 178,* 172-179.

Herbert, J., & Mueser, K. (1992). Eye movement desensitization: A critique of the evidence. *Journal of Behavior Therapy and Experimental Psychiatry, 23,* 169-174.

Hodgson, R. J., & Rachman, S. (1977). Obsessional compulsive complaints. *Behaviour Research and Therapy, 15,* 389-395.

Holt, C., Heimberg, R., & Hope, D. (1992). Avoidant personality disorder and the generalized subtype of social phobia. *Journal of Abnormal Psychology, 101,* 318-325.

Insel, T. (1982). Obsessive compulsive disorder--Five clinical questions and a suggested approach. *Comprehensive Psychiatry, 23,* 241-251.

Jenike, M. (1983). Obsessive-compulsive disorder. *Comprehensive Psychiatry, 24,* 99-115.

Jenike, M., Baer, L., & Minichiello, W. (1987). Somatic treatments for obsessive-compulsive disorders. *Comprehensive Psychiatry, 28,* 250-263.

Jenike, M., Baer, L., Minichiello, W., Schwartz, C., & Carey, R. (1986). Concomitant obsessive-compulsive disorder and schizotypal personality disorder. *American Journal of Psychiatry, 143,* 530-532.

Jerremalm, A., Jansson, L., & Öst, L.-G. (1986). Cognitive and physiological reactivity and the effects of different behavioral methods in the treatment of social phobia. *Behaviour Research and Therapy, 24,* 171-180.

Johnson, S. B. (1985). Situational fears and object phobias. In D. Shaffer, A. Ehrhardt, & L. Greenhill (Eds.), *The Guide to Child Psychiatry* (pp. 169-181). New York: Free Press.

Jones, J. C., & Barlow, D. (1990). The etiology of posttraumatic stress disorder. *Clinical Psychology Review, 10,* 299-328.

Kearney, C., & Silverman, W. (1992). Let's not push the panic button: A critical analysis of panic and panic disorder in adolescents. *Clinical Psychology Review, 12,* 293-305.

Keller, M., & Baker, L. (1992). The clinical course of panic disorder and depression. *Journal of Clinical Psychiatry, 53*(Suppl. 3), 5-8.

Kendall, P., Kortlander, E., Chanansky, T., & Brady, U. (1992). Comorbidity of anxiety and depression in youth: Treatment implications. *Journal of Consulting and Clinical Psychology, 60,* 869-880.

Kinzie, J. D., & Boehnlein, J. (1989). Post-traumatic psychosis among Cambodian refugees. *Journal of Traumatic Stress, 2,* 185-198.

Klass, E. T., DiNardo, P., & Barlow, D. (1989). DSM-III-R personality diagnoses in anxiety disorder patients. *Comprehensive Psychiatry, 30,* 251-258.

Knapp, S., & VandeCreek, L. (1988). A clinician's guide to popular anxiety books. *Private Practice of Psychotherapy, 6,* 17-39.

Koeppen, A. S. (1974). Relaxation training for children. *Elementary School Guidance and Counseling, 9,* 14-21.

Krystal, H. (1968). *Massive Psychic Trauma.* New York: International Universities Press.

Lange, A., & Jukubowski, R. (1976). *Responsible Assertive Behavior: Cognitive Behavioral Procedures for Trainers.* Champaign, IL: Research Press.

Last, C., Francis, G., Hersen, M., Kazdin, A., & Strauss, C. (1987). Separation anxiety and school phobia: A comparison using DSM-III criteria. *American Journal of Psychiatry, 144,* 652-653.

Lazarus, A. (1976). *Multimodal Behavior Therapy.* New York: Springer.

Lehrer, P., & Woolfolk, R. (1984). Are stress reduction techniques interchangeable, or do they have specific effects? A review of the comparative empirical literature. In R. Woolfolk & P. Lehrer (Eds.), *Principles and Practice of Stress Management* (pp. 404-477). New York: Guilford.

Liebowitz, M., Campeas, R., Levin, A., Sandberg, D., Hollander, E., & Papp, L. (1987). Pharmacotherapy of social phobia. *Psychosomatics, 28,* 305-308.

Liebowitz, M., Gorman, J., Fyer, A., & Klein, D. (1985). Social phobia: Review of a neglected disorder. *Archives of General Psychiatry, 42,* 729-736.

Lifton, R. (1973). *Home from the War: Vietnam Veterans: Neither Victims Nor Executioners.* New York: Simon & Shuster.

Lyons, J., & Keane, T. (1989). Implosive therapy for the treatment of combat related PTSD. *Journal of Traumatic Stress, 2,* 137-152.

Markowitz, J., Weissman, M., Ouellette, R., Lish, J., & Klerman, G. (1989). Quality of life in panic disorder. *Archives of General Psychiatry, 46,* 984-992.

Marks, I. (1978). *Living with Fear.* New York: McGraw-Hill.

Marks, I. (1985). Behavioral treatment of social phobia. *Psychopharmacology Bulletin, 21,* 615-618.

Marks, I. (1987). *Fears, Phobias, and Rituals: Panic, Anxiety, and Their Disorders.* New York: Oxford University Press.

Marks, I., & Matthews, A. (1979). Brief standard self-rating for phobic patients. *Behaviour Research and Therapy, 17,* 263-267.

Marquis, J. (1991). A report on seventy-eight cases treated by eye-movement desensitization. *Journal of Behavior Therapy and Experimental Psychiatry, 22,* 187-192.

Marshall, J. (1993). Social phobia: An overview of treatment strategies. *Journal of Clinical Psychiatry, 54,* 165-171.

Massion, A., Warshaw, M., & Keller, M. (1993). Quality of life and psychiatric morbidity in panic disorder and generalized anxiety disorder. *American Journal of Psychiatry, 150,* 600-607.

Mauri, M., Sarno, N., Rossi, V., Armani, A., Zambotto, S., Cassano, G., & Akiskal, H. (1992). Personality disorders associated with generalized anxiety, panic, and recurrent major depression. *Journal of Personality Disorders, 6,* 162-167.

Mavissakalian, M., & Hamann, M. S. (1986). DSM-III personality disorder in agoraphobia. *Comprehensive Psychiatry, 27,* 471-479.

Mavissakalian, M., & Hamann, M. S. (1987). DSM-III personality disorder in agoraphobia II: Changes with treatment. *Comprehensive Psychiatry, 28,* 356-361.

Mavissakalian, M., & Hamann, M. S. (1988). Correlates of DSM-III personality disorder in panic disorder and agoraphobia. *Comprehensive Psychiatry, 29,* 535-544.

Mavissakalian, M., & Hamann, M. S. (1992). DSM-III personality characteristics of panic disorder with agoraphobia patients in stable remission. *Comprehensive Psychiatry, 33,* 305-309.

Mavissakalian, M., Hamann, M. S., & Jones, B. (1990). A comparison of DSM-III personality disorders in panic/agoraphobia and obsessive-compulsive disorders. *Comprehensive Psychiatry, 31,* 238-244.

Mavissakalian, M., Turner, S., Michelson, L., & Jacob, R. (1985). Tricyclic antidepressants in obsessive-compulsive disorder: Antiobsessional or antidepressant agents?: II. *American Journal of Psychiatry, 142*, 572-576.

McCann, B., Woolfolk, R., & Lehrer, P. (1987). Specificity in response to treatment: A study of interpersonal anxiety. *Behaviour Research and Therapy, 25*, 129-136.

Meichenbaum, D. (1977). *Cognitive Behavior Modification.* New York: Plenum.

Mersh, P., Emmelkamp, P., Bogels, S., & Van der Sleen, J. (1989). Social phobia: Individual response patterns and the effects of behavioral and cognitive interventions. *Behaviour Research and Therapy, 27*, 421-434.

Michelson, L. (1987). Cognitive-behavioral assessment and treatment of agoraphobia. In L. Michelson & L. M. Ascher (Eds.), *Anxiety and Stress Disorders* (pp. 213-279). New York: Guilford.

Michelson, L., & Ascher, L. M. (1984). Paradoxical intention in the treatment of agoraphobia and other anxiety disorders. *Journal of Behavior Therapy and Experimental Psychiatry, 15*, 215-220.

Michelson, L., & Marchione, K. (1991). Behavioral, cognitive and pharmacological treatments of panic disorder with agoraphobia: Critique and synthesis. *Journal of Consulting and Clinical Psychology, 59*, 100-114.

Millon, T. (1982). *Millon Clinical Multiaxial Inventory Manual.* Minneapolis: National Computer Systems.

Myers, J., Weissman, M., Tischler, G., Holzer, C., Leaf, P., Orvaschel, H., Anthony, J., Boyd, J., Burke, J., Kramer, M., & Stoltzman, R. (1984). Six-month prevalence of psychiatric disorders in three communities. *Archives of General Psychiatry, 41*, 959-967.

Neal, A., & Turner, S. (1991). Anxiety disorders research with African Americans: Current status. *Psychological Bulletin, 109*, 400-410.

Nelles, W. B., & Barlow, D. (1988). Do children panic? *Clinical Psychology Review, 8*, 359-372.

Nelson, R. O., & Barlow, D. (1984). Behavioral assessment: Basic strategies and initial procedures. In D. Barlow (Ed.),

Behavioral Assessment of Adult Disorders (pp. 13-44). New York: Guilford.

Neuman, F. (1985). *Fighting Fear.* New York: Bantam.

Norton, G., Cox, B., & Schwartz, M. (1992). Critical analysis of the DSM-III-R classification of panic disorder: A survey of current opinions. *Journal of Anxiety Disorders, 6,* 159-167.

Norton, G., Harrison, B., Hauch, J., & Rhodes, L. (1985). Characteristics of people with infrequent panic attacks. *Journal of Abnormal Psychology, 94,* 216-221.

Öst, L.-G. (1985). Ways of acquiring phobia and outcome of behavioral treatments. *Behaviour Research and Therapy, 23,* 683-689.

Öst, L.-G. (1992). Blood and injection phobia: Background and cognitive, physiological, and behavioral variables. *Journal of Abnormal Psychology, 101,* 68-74.

Öst, L.-G., & Hugdahl, K. (1981). Acquisition of phobia and anxiety response patterns in clinical patients. *Behaviour Research and Therapy, 19,* 439-444.

Öst, L.-G., Jerremalm, A., & Johansson, J. (1981). Individual response patterns and the effects of different behavioral methods in the treatment of social phobia. *Behaviour Research and Therapy, 19*(1), 1-16.

Öst, L.-G., Johansson, J., & Jerremalm, A. (1982). Individual response patterns and the effects of different behavioral methods in the treatment of claustrophobia. *Behaviour Research and Therapy, 20,* 445-460.

Öst, L.-G., & Sterner, U. (1987). Applied tension: A specific behavioral method for treatment of blood phobia. *Behaviour Research and Therapy, 25,* 25-29.

Öst, L.-G., Sterner, U., & Fellenius, J. (1989). Applied tension, applied relaxation, and the combination in the treatment of blood phobia. *Behaviour Research and Therapy, 27,* 109-121.

Paul, G. (1966). *Insight Versus Desensitization.* Stanford: Stanford University Press.

Pfohl, B., & Blum, N. (1991). Obsessive-compulsive personality disorder: A review of available data and recommendations for DSM-IV. *Journal of Personality Disorders, 5,* 363-375.

Pollack, M., Otto, M., Rosenbaum, J., & Sachs, G. (1992). Personality disorders in patients with panic disorder: Association with childhood anxiety disorders, early trauma, comorbidity, and chronicity. *Comprehensive Psychiatry, 33,* 78-83.

Questions and answers. (1993). *Journal of Clinical Psychiatry, 54,* 39-41.

Rachman, S. (1974). Primary obsessional slowness. *Behaviour Research and Therapy, 12,* 9-18.

Rachman, S. (1989). The return of fear: Review and prospect. *Clinical Psychology Review, 9,* 147-168.

Rachman, S. (1990). *Fear and Courage* (2nd ed.). San Francisco: Freeman.

Rapee, R. M. (1991). Generalized anxiety disorder: A review of clinical features and theoretical concepts. *Clinical Psychology Review, 11,* 419-440.

Raphael, B. (1986). *When Disaster Strikes.* New York: Basic Books.

Rapoport, J. (1985). Childhood obsessive-compulsive disorder. In D. Shaffer, A. Ehrhardt, & L. Greenhill (Eds.), *The Clinical Guide To Child Psychiatry.* New York: Free Press.

Rapoport, J., Swedo, S., & Leonard, H. (1992). Childhood obsessive compulsive disorder. *Journal of Clinical Psychiatry, 53*(Suppl. 4), 11-16.

Rasmussen, S., & Eisen, J. (1992). The epidemiology and differential diagnosis of obsessive compulsive disorder. *Journal of Clinical Psychiatry, 53*(Suppl. 4), 4-9.

Rasmussen, S., & Tsuang, M. (1986). Clinical characteristics and family history in DSM-III obsessive-compulsive disorder. *American Journal of Psychiatry, 143,* 317-322.

Reich, J. (1986). The epidemiology of anxiety. *The Journal of Nervous and Mental Disease, 174,* 129-136.

Robins, L., Helzer, J., Weissman, M., Orvaschel, H., Gruenberg, E., Burke, J., & Regier, D. (1984). Lifetime prevalence of specific psychiatric disorders in three sites. *Archives of General Psychiatry, 41,* 949-958.

Sanderson, W., DiNardo, P., Rapee, R. M., & Barlow, D. (1990). Syndrome comorbidity in patients diagnosed with a DSM-III-R anxiety disorder. *Journal of Abnormal Psychology, 99,* 308-312.

Sarafino, E. (1986). *The Fears of Childhood*. New York: Human Sciences Press.

Schneier, F. (1991). Social phobia. *Psychiatric Annals, 21,* 349-353.

Schwartz, G., Davidson, R., & Coleman, D. (1978). Patterning of cognitive and somatic processes in the self-regulation of anxiety: Effects of meditation versus exercise. *Psychosomatic Medicine, 40,* 321-328.

Shapiro, F. (1989). Efficacy of the Eye Movement Desensitization Procedure in the treatment of traumatic memories. *Journal of Traumatic Stress, 2,* 199-224.

Shapiro, F. (1993). Eye Movement Desensitization and Reprocessing (EMDR) in 1992. *Journal of Traumatic Stress, 6,* 417-422.

Shea, M. T. (1993). Psychosocial treatment of personality disorders. *Journal of Personality Disorders, 7*(Spring Suppl.), 167-180.

Shear, M. K., Cooper, A., Klerman, G., Busch, F., & Shapiro, T. (1993). A psychodynamic model of panic disorder. *American Journal of Psychiatry, 150,* 859-866.

Sheehan, D. (1984). *The Anxiety Disease*. Toronto: Bantam.

Shipley, R., & Boudewyns, P. (1980). Flooding and implosive therapy: Are they harmful? *Behavior Therapy, 11,* 503-508.

Smith, T. (1982). Irrational beliefs in the cause and treatment of emotional distress: A critical review of the rational-emotive model. *Clinical Psychology Review, 2,* 505-510.

Somnier, F., & Genefke, I. (1986). Psychotherapy for victims of torture. *British Journal of Psychiatry, 149,* 323-329.

Spielberger, C. D., Gorsuch, R. L., & Lushene, R. (1970). *The State-Trait Anxiety Inventory*. Palo Alto, CA: Consulting Psychologists Press.

Stanley, M., Turner, S., & Borden, J. (1989, August). Schizotypal Features in Obsessive-Compulsive Disorder. Paper presented at the American Psychological Association Convention, New Orleans, LA.

Stein, D., Hollander, E., & Skodol, A. (1993). Anxiety disorders and personality disorders: A review. *Journal of Personality Disorders, 7,* 87-102.

Stein, M. (1986). Panic disorder and medical illness. *Psychosomatics, 27,* 833-838.

Steketee, G., & Foa, E. (1985). Obsessive-compulsive disorder. In D. Barlow (Ed.), *Clinical Handbook of Psychological Disorders* (pp 69-144). New York: Guilford.

Stravynski, A., Lamontagne, Y., & Lavallee, Y.-J. (1986). Clinical phobias and avoidant personality disorder among alcoholics admitted to an alcoholism rehabilitation setting. *Canadian Journal of Psychiatry, 31,* 714-719.

Suinn, R. (1977). *Manual for Anxiety Management Training.* Fort Collins, CO: Rocky Mountain Behavioral Science Institute.

Sweet, A., Giles, T., & Young, R. (1987). Three theoretical perspectives on anxiety: A comparison of theory and outcome. In L. Michelson & L. M. Ascher (Eds.), *Anxiety and Stress Disorders* (pp. 39-61). New York: Guilford.

Thyer, B., Himle, J., & Curtis, G. (1985). Blood-injury illness phobia: A review. *Journal of Clinical Psychology, 41,* 451-459.

Thyer, B., Parrish, R., Curtis, G., Neese, R., & Cameron, O. (1985). Ages of onset of DSM-III anxiety disorders. *Comprehensive Psychiatry, 26,* 113-122.

Titchener, J., & Kapp, F. (1976). Family and character change at Buffalo Creek. *American Journal of Psychiatry, 133,* 295-299.

Turner, S., & Beidel, D. (1985). Empirically derived subtypes of social anxiety. *Behavior Therapy, 16,* 384-392.

Turner, S., Beidel, D., Borden, J., Stanley, M., & Jacob, R. (1991). Social phobia: Axis I and II correlates. *Journal of Abnormal Psychology, 100,* 102-106.

Turner, S., Beidel, D., Dancu, C., & Keys, D. (1986). Psychopathology of social phobia and comparison to avoidant personality disorder. *Journal of Abnormal Psychology, 95,* 389-394.

Turner, S., McCann, B., Beidel, D., & Mezzich, J. (1986). DSM-III classification of anxiety disorders: A psychometric study. *Journal of Abnormal Psychology, 95,* 168-172.

Turner, S., & Michelson, L. (1984). Obsessive-compulsive disorder. In S. Turner (Ed.), *Behavioral Theories and Treatment of Anxiety* (pp. 239-278). New York: Plenum.

Turner, S., Williams, S. L., Beidel, D., & Mezzich, J. (1986). Panic disorder and agoraphobia with panic attacks: Covariation along the dimensions of panic and agoraphobic fear. *Journal of Abnormal Psychology, 95,* 384-388.

Van Devanter, L., & Morgan, C. (1984). *Home Before Morning.* New York: Warner.

Veale, D. (1993). Classification and treatment of obsessional slowness. *British Journal of Psychiatry, 162,* 198-203.

Weekes, C. (1969). *Hope and Help for Your Nerves.* New York: Bantam.

Weekes, C. (1976). *Peace from Nervous Suffering.* New York: Bantam.

Weekes, C. (1984). *More Hope and Help for Your Nerves.* New York: Bantam.

Weissman, M. (1993). The epidemiology of personality disorders. *Journal of Personality Disorders, 7*(Spring Suppl.), 44-62.

Weissman, M., Leaf, P., Holzer, C., & Merikangas, K. (1985). Panic disorder and major depression: Epidemiology, family studies, biologic, and treatment response similarities. *Psychopharmacology Bulletin, 21,* 538-541.

Wells, S. (1984). Caffeine: Implications of recent research for clinical practice. *American Journal of Orthopsychiatry, 54,* 375-389.

Whalen, S., DiGiuseppe, R., & Wessler, R. (1980). *A Practitioners Guide to Rational-Emotive Therapy.* New York: Oxford University Press.

Williams, J. (1987). Revised classification for anxiety disorders. *Hospital and Community Psychiatry, 38,* 245-246.

Wolpe, J. (1977). Inadequate behavior analysis: The Achilles Heel of outcome research in behavior therapy. *Journal of Behavior Therapy and Experimental Psychiatry, 8*(1), 1-3.

Wolpe, J. (1981). The dichotomy between classical conditioned and cognitively learned anxiety. *Journal of Behavior Therapy and Experimental Psychiatry, 12,* 35-42.

Wolpe, J. (1990). *The Practice of Behavior Therapy* (4th ed.). New York: Pergamon.

Wolpe, J., & Lang, P. (1969). *Fear Survey Schedule.* San Diego, CA: Educational and Industrial Testing.

Woolfolk, R., & Lehrer, P. (Eds.). (1984). *Principles and Practice of Stress Management.* New York: Guilford.

Zane, M., & Milt, H. (1984). *Your Phobia.* New York: Warner.

If You Found This Book Useful . . .

You might want to know more about our other titles.

For a complete listing of our publications, please write, call, or fax the following information to the address and phone number listed below:

Name:_____
(Please print)

Address:_____

Address:_____

City/State/Zip:_____

Telephone:(_____)_____

I am a:

_____ Psychologist   _____ Mental Health Counselor
_____ Psychiatrist   _____ Marriage and Family Therapist
_____ School Psychologist   _____ Not in Mental Health Field
_____ Clinical Social Worker   _____ Other:_____

♦   ♦   ♦

Professional Resource Press
P.O. Box 15560
Sarasota, FL 34277-1560

Telephone #813-366-7913
FAX #813-366-7971

Add A Colleague To Our Mailing List . . .

If you would like us to send our latest catalog to one of your colleagues, please return this form.

Name:_____
(Please print)

Address:_____

Address:_____

City/State/Zip:_____

Telephone:(_____)_____

I am a:

_____ Psychologist   _____ Mental Health Counselor
_____ Psychiatrist   _____ Marriage and Family Therapist
_____ School Psychologist   _____ Not in Mental Health Field
_____ Clinical Social Worker   _____ Other:_____

♦   ♦   ♦

Professional Resource Press
P.O. Box 15560
Sarasota, FL 34277-1560

Telephone #813-366-7913
FAX #813-366-7971

Add A Colleague To Our Mailing List . . .

If you would like us to send our latest catalog to one of your colleagues, please return this form.

Name:_____
(Please print)

Address:_____

Address:_____

City/State/Zip:_____

Telephone:(_____)_____

I am a:

_____ Psychologist   _____ Mental Health Counselor
_____ Psychiatrist   _____ Marriage and Family Therapist
_____ School Psychologist   _____ Not in Mental Health Field
_____ Clinical Social Worker   _____ Other:_____

◆   ◆   ◆

Professional Resource Press
P.O. Box 15560
Sarasota, FL 34277-1560

Telephone #813-366-7913
FAX #813-366-7971

If You Found This Book Useful . . .

You might want to know more about our other titles.

For a complete listing of our publications, please write, call, or fax the following information to the address and phone number listed below:

Name:_____
(Please print)

Address:_____

Address:_____

City/State/Zip:_____

Telephone:(_____)_____

I am a:

_____ Psychologist	_____ Mental Health Counselor
_____ Psychiatrist	_____ Marriage and Family Therapist
_____ School Psychologist	_____ Not in Mental Health Field
_____ Clinical Social Worker	_____ Other:_____

◆   ◆   ◆

Professional Resource Press
P.O. Box 15560
Sarasota, FL 34277-1560

Telephone #813-366-7913
FAX #813-366-7971

501262